Timeless Waters

MaaWää'Ta':
A Story to be Written

a novel by

Sheryl L. Marseilles

ISBN: 978-0-578-00423-5

Copyright © 2008 by Sheryl Marseilles

sherylmarseilles@yahoo.com

Cover art and illustrations by Jennifer Hunter

To Marilyn
For Sharing the Journey

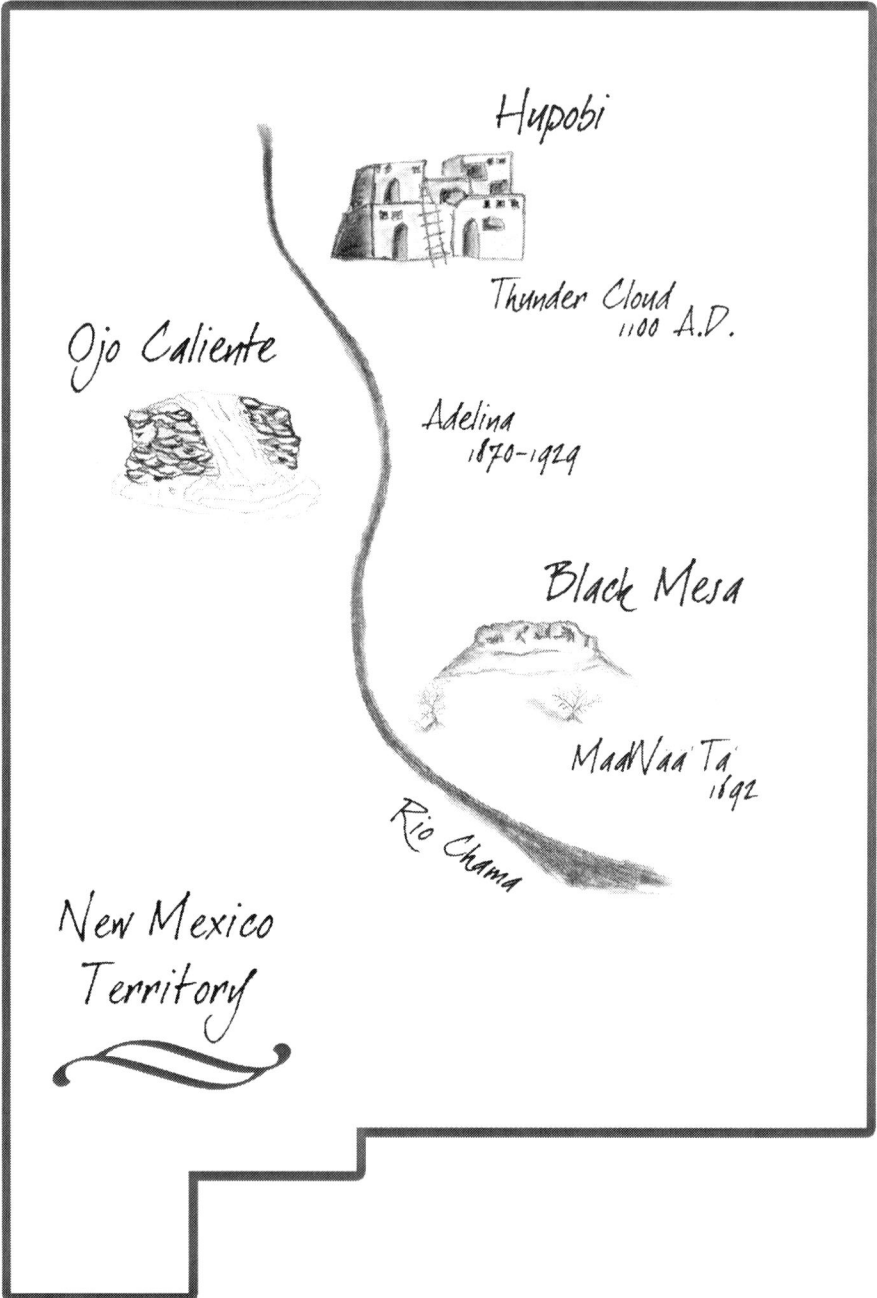

Hupobi

Thunder Cloud
1100 A.D.

Ojo Caliente

Adelina
1870-1929

Black Mesa

MaaNaa'Tá
1692

Rio Chama

New Mexico
Territory

Introduction

There have been times when I have questioned what my life would be like if I hadn't taken the career, wife and mommy path. This isn't because I regret my choices, but because there has always been a part of me that yearned for something else too: a life of freedom and adventure, unencumbered, and going where the wind takes me.

But there are forms of adventure of which I was only somewhat aware of in my younger years. These are the journeys that, for lack of a better description, are the opposite of thrusting one's self outward; they are quiet, perhaps even unobservable to the outside world. So subtle are these adventures that it is only at the end of one that you fully grasp its magnitude.

I sat one cold Sunday morning with my chair pulled up to the fireplace. My cat's gray and tan color blended perfectly with the stone hearth where she lay with her head propped on my feet, sharing the warmth of the blaze. I closed my eyes and started to drift in my thoughts. One floated into the next with little effort or intention. An image appeared on the screen of darkness behind my closed eyes—it was a woman. As I caught a glimpse of her and pondered her familiarity, her blue eyes locked with mine for just a moment. Then, as quickly as it flashed before me, the image faded away. When I opened my eyes, I turned to look over my shoulder, half expecting to see her there.

That was our first meeting, and there would be many more. She would reach out to me as I went about the mundane— when I woke from sleep, as I walked through the grocery store, or drove the kids to school. She moved through me, and as she did, I came to know her. Over time, there were others that reached out to me as she did, and a story interwoven across space and time was revealed.

I have often found myself wondering how the events I wish to share with you are possible and why they might have occurred, to me, of all people. As I ask those questions, my memory repeatedly takes me to a moment years ago when I stood in front of a shelf of books at the book store. I was looking for something— something that might light a spark I knew lay within me or some words of inspiration that would help me shed the baggage that burdened my life and relationships. I closed my eyes, there in the Self Help section of Barnes and Noble, and silently asked for wholeness.

They say when the student is ready, the teacher appears. I must have been ready, because mine appeared and I imagine I will never be the same. They sought me out, showed me their lives, and through them I faced myself. It is a story worth telling and one I wish to share with you.

Louisa

1

She stands outside the small adobe, arms folded tightly over her chest, and surveys the tree spotted mountains. She hears the rush of the river and closes her eyes, feeling the breeze as it blows across her skin.

Her thoughts turn inward, and on the edges of her numbness she feels loneliness and loss. Looking up at the blue sky, she recalls the countless nights of looking at the stars, waiting patiently for something in her life to change and the change never coming.

She turns and walks into the one room house. The early afternoon sun shines through the small window next to her and she feels its warmth on her shoulders. The solitude of her life overwhelms her and her gift of numbness is gone.

Tears stream down her face. She looks at her feet as she steps up and places the noose around her neck. She calls to the God whom she long ago lost faith in and steps off.

* * * *

She awoke with a gasp- her heart pounding. Her throat constricted and her chest was tight like when she had asthma as a child. Was she having an attack? It had been years. Confused about what was happening, Louisa fumbled for the old inhaler she kept in the night table. She put it in her mouth and took a deep breath, thankful she still had one around for emergencies. Settling back into the mounds of pillows that surrounded her warm spot in the bed, she could hear the winter wind pushing against the windows as she looked at the early morning light against the sage green walls. As she recalled her dream, it seemed familiar. She couldn't shake the sense of isolation and hopelessness. *Have I had that dream before?*

As she began to wake up, she realized there was a small foot under her pillow and she felt her two sons stirring in the bed next to her. She wrapped her hand around the foot and, slowly sitting up, looked over and saw three-year-old Isaac and nine-month-old Caleb. Her husband was asleep on the other side of the boys. *He made it off the couch I see.* She crawled out of bed and walked over to him, giving him a nudge. "It's almost seven. I'm getting in the shower," she said quietly. "You're in charge of the baby." Alan mumbled and rolled over, going back to sleep.

She flipped on the bathroom light and turned on the hot water in the shower, then looked at herself in the mirror as she pulled the band out of her chestnut brown hair, allowing it to fall to her shoulders. *Damn I look tired,* she said to herself as she noted the dark circles around her blue eyes. She pulled off her flannel pajama bottoms and t-shirt then turned to the side, sucking in what remained of her "baby weight." About five pounds left. *Patience.*

Checking the temperature of the water, Louisa stepped into the shower and let the steamy heat clear the cobwebs from her head. While she was rinsing her hair, she heard Isaac's small voice, "Mommy?"

She quickly grabbed a towel and stepped out to greet her son. "How's my angel boy? Come over here and give me some hugs," she said. She knelt down and he wrapped his arms around her.

The morning progressed in all the normal chaos, and as Louisa drove to the office, she noted that Christmas was ten days away and she wouldn't have childcare for the next two weeks. "Attitude is everything," she told herself, putting on a smile and preparing for cold weather and being trapped in the house. She practiced smiling when her attitude was bad, believing on some level the act itself would fool her brain and she'd actually *feel* happy. As the Executive Director of a child advocacy organization charged with representing the best interests of abused and neglected children who were wards of the court, work, while a definite stressor in her life, was a stressor she didn't want to be without. Not only did it provide an income, but due to the amount of intellectual stimulation she required, it provided sanity as well. Before their second child, Caleb, was born, she and Alan had talked about the possibility of her staying home, knowing that child care for two kids would be costly. "I think it would be in everyone's best interest if you keep working," Alan had joked, implying she would go bonkers if she chose to stay at home. As she turned into the parking lot, she smiled to herself that he was probably right.

The day at the office was a relatively quiet one. She finished the budget for the next fiscal year, did some preliminary work on a grant due the following month and staffed some cases with Reed, one of her caseworkers. After wrapping up some loose ends, she left to pick up the kids at their nursery school.

As she drove home, she noticed the sun was setting early and remembered the Winter Solstice was coming up. Louisa commented on the streaked sky and pointed out the colors to Isaac, sitting in the back seat. They made their way into their neighborhood east of town, and as they rounded the last curve in the road, the vibrant pink sky cast a reflection off the small lake behind their stone and cedar shingle home. She turned down the steep driveway and pulled the car into the garage. With full arms, of baby and diaper bag to artwork and a pair of green lizard snow boots worn that morning but impractical for running on the playground, she made her way into the house.

She passed through the utility room and dropped Isaac's boots and artwork on the dryer. Caleb wiggled to be released from Louisa's hold and she gently set him on the floor. Stepping over him as he crawled, she flipped the light switch in the kitchen that opened up into the living room.

Isaac stood next to the Christmas tree playing with the ornaments, which were actually small toys from his toy box. "Sweetheart, do you want to watch Rudolph?" she asked him.

"Rudolph!" he yelled and ran over to the couch.

Louisa plugged in the tree lights and put three small logs in the fireplace. "You stay put while I light this okay? And holler if Caleb starts to crawl over here." She held the lighter and turned on the gas until she heard the crackle of burning wood. "Okay babe," she said, inserting the video and walking over to kiss his head. "I'll be right back."

She put Caleb in the baby-sling that hung over the back of the chair and made her way into the kitchen. As she turned the small plastic knob on the box of chardonnay in the refrigerator, the phone started to ring. Putting the glass of wine down on the counter, she steadied her son's body in the sling and ran to answer the phone.

"Hello?" she answered, plopping down in the green, overstuffed chair next to the front window.

"Hey sweetie. What are ya' doing?" It was her friend, Malory. "I need to give you a heads-up on something," she said.

"Well, right now I'm taking Caleb out of the sling and putting him on the floor, and, there he goes, crawling away. What's up?" she asked as she repositioned herself in the chair and picked some dog hair out of the Zapotec rug that was draped across the back.

"Well, it's your husband. He's up to something. He's really trying to be very kind to you, but I think you may need a warning."

"Okay. What's he trying to do?" Louisa asked, shifting in the chair so she could look at the Christmas lights in the bushes just outside the front window.

"Well, he called me the other day and said he wanted to send you away with a friend for your Christmas present."

Alan was coming through for her again; she was lucky in that sense. Yet, wondering why she needed a heads up, she responded pensively. "Okay."

Malory continued. "So, you and I are going to Ojo Caliente, New Mexico the first week of January."

"You mean in two weeks?" asked Louisa, the panic obvious in her voice. "What is he thinking? Doesn't he realize I might need some warning? I just stopped breast feeding. Leaving the kids takes mental preparation."

"I know, I know. That's why I called to warn you, so you won't panic and can act happy when he tells you," said Malory.

Louisa took a deep breath. "Okay, now where are we going again?"

"Ojo Caliente, New Mexico. He said you two stopped there right after you were married. He was adamant that you love it there…and it really is a nice gesture."

Louisa hung up the phone after agreeing to talk to Malory the next day. She vaguely remembered this place in New Mexico and found it interesting that Alan thought she loved it there. One of his nicknames for her was "vacation junkie," which was somewhat accurate, so getting away anywhere was great with her. She wandered back into the kitchen to fetch her glass of wine and leaned on the counter as she took a small sip. She watched Isaac pull his little brother on the couch and the two sat side by side.

She took another sip from her glass and smiled to herself. She had a good life, didn't she? Her two babies cuddling on the couch, a warm fire burning, a comfortable home surrounded by nature, a job she loved, and a husband sending her away with a friend for her Christmas present. It was gestures like that from Alan that kept Louisa hanging in there, in spite of how difficult their marriage had been. But it had been a good year—the best for them so far. There was much to be thankful for.

2

The chaos of the holiday week passed and she would be leaving town in a few days. Louisa lay with Isaac, patting him to sleep. She snuggled up next to him on the twin size bed and watched him as he gazed at the shapes the nightlight cast on the ceiling. "Hush, sweet angel," she whispered, stroking his head.

Isaac started to relax and his eyes began to slowly close. Their hair, matching in color, commingled as it splashed across the pillow, making it difficult to tell where his ended and hers began. Louisa took a deep breath, smelling the Baby Magic shampoo used earlier that night, and closed her eyes.

She drifted off to sleep and was overcome by a peaceful feeling that something was going to happen to her while she was gone. She sat up, jerking herself awake. Was something going to happen—an accident of some kind? She struggled to recall what thoughts or images were in her mind before she woke up. Her peaceful reaction alarmed her. Was she okay with something happening? Trying to shake it off, she bent over to kiss Isaac's forehead and went on to bed.

The following day, she stood rinsing the breakfast dishes in front of the kitchen sink. The trees filtered the morning sun as it made its way through the large windows, dabbling the terracotta walls. As she rinsed the last plate, she glanced out at the birdfeeder hanging from the bare branch of a pecan tree. There were two cardinals perched there, a male and female, and she smiled as she commented to herself that you rarely saw one without the other. She heard a "thud," bringing back her focus, and looked to see Caleb's sippy cup on the floor.

"Are you ready to get out of that high chair, pumpkin?" she asked, walking toward him. He squealed and pounded his small hands on the tray, flashing a semi-toothed smile. "Okay little man." She smiled, grabbed the wash cloth off the counter and wiped his face.

Louisa lifted him out of the chair, nuzzled his nose with hers and stared into his laughing brown eyes. He grabbed two fist-fulls of hair and put his mouth over her chin, biting down in an affectionate baby-style kiss. As she held him close, her thoughts turned back to her anxiety the night before, and a subtle panic coursed through her veins. She took a deep breath to calm herself, and as she did, she recalled a fascinating experience she had when she was pregnant with him.

One of her coworkers had experienced a death in her family. Knowing Reed was open minded, Louisa suggested she and her husband, Daniel, go with her to a "Spirit Expo" in Oklahoma City. There was a woman Louisa had heard about who could access "other realms" psychically and could communicate with people who had crossed to "the other side."

When they arrived, the room was packed with more than a hundred people. There were only a few chairs available in the back rows, so Louisa took a seat behind her friends. Everyone was given a piece of paper and the group was told to write the name of who they wanted to contact or a question they wanted answered, to fold the paper and to write their names on the outside. Louisa didn't have a question since she was there for Reed and Daniel, and quite frankly, was just happy to be sitting in a chair rather than being seven months pregnant and standing in the back. She folded her slip of paper, put it in her pocket, and waited while the questions were collected and placed in a basket. Cyndy, the psychic, began preparing for the session. She turned on some music, put on a blindfold, and appeared to be getting herself centered. When she was ready, she told the group she would simply say what came to her, so if it sounded like something that applied to you, to speak up.

Cyndy gestured with her finger. "I see a small light like a star. It's coming down, and going back up. It's small," she continued, holding her hands about a foot apart. "Is someone here pregnant?"

Louisa sat quietly, waiting to see if anyone spoke up. Reed turned and slapped Louisa's leg, causing her to jump.

"Say something," whispered Reed, turning around to look at her.

"Alright," Louisa mouthed silently to Reed. "I'm pregnant," she called out, tugging on Reed's hair. Reed snickered and reached back, swatting Louisa's leg again.

"Is your name Louise?" she asked.

"It's Louisa," she responded from the back of the room.

"Okay, Louisa. Caleb is here."

Daniel turned and looked at Louisa, open mouthed. She had just told him on the drive up that they had decided last week to name the baby Caleb. Louisa sat in amazement and the psychic continued. "He doesn't really seem to have anything specific to say, except he's full of joy and he's ready to be with you."

After recalling the experience, Louisa determined she was panicked enough, and just neurotic enough, to look outside herself for reassurance that she would return home safely. She transferred Caleb's weight to her hip and walked over to the "miscellaneous" drawer in her kitchen where she had saved a brochure from the Spirit Expo. She dug around until she saw it.

"Let's see here little man," she said to Caleb as she looked over the brochure. "Here it is. 'On-line readings.' I wonder how that works if the person isn't physically present?"

Caleb pulled the purple brochure out of her hand and put it in his mouth. "Well, if she had contact with you before you were born, anything's possible, right?" She kissed his head and took the slobbery piece of paper, fishing a missing corner out of his mouth with her finger.

After putting Caleb down, Louisa walked to her computer and e-mailed the psychic. She told her she was going on a trip to New Mexico and wanted to know if she would return home safely. Two days later, the day before she was leaving, Louisa got her response.

> *"Hi Louisa.*
>
> *This is Cyndy responding to your online question. I get pictures and images in no particular order. I will tell you the information, and you use your own intuition to put them where they belong. Take what feels right and don't worry about the rest. It may come to you*

later, or I may have not interpreted it right in the first place.

Ok...

First, this year 2002 is a great, wonderful, powerful year for you and Spirit (God, your angels, your guides or whatever term you want to use). A powerful year for your spiritual growth, foundation, and ability to trust that Spirit is in fact communicating with you. So know that and use this year to work toward that goal. You are intuitive naturally, but the problem is your logical brain works overtime. Very much like a man's...logical and thinking all the time. So when you have those intuitive moments, I see that logic immediately says, "Well, it could have been the wind," "Well, it was a lucky guess," etc. You end up talking yourself out of the intuitive moments.

Your goal this year is to quiet the logic in your mind and to learn to trust the intuitive just as much—which is hard because, for 30-35 years, logic has ruled and now we must teach it does not. It is a balance of logic and intuition that will keep you at peace.

Spirit says this is a year of spiritual studies and getting more solid in your knowing they are with you and speaking to you. More assured that it is spirit you are hearing. So ask them for signs, such as "when you are with me, I will feel the wind on my face, or I will feel you on my right." Something that you can begin to pay attention to and look for and trust they are there and listen. Spirit says in the past you have been frustrated or dissatisfied in the way they have come to you. Example: I want to see spirit. Well maybe you don't see them, you feel them instead. Or: I want to hear a loud voice. Maybe you don't hear a loud voice, maybe you have instant knowingness instead.

Anyhow, Spirit is communicating. Quit being picky about how and just acknowledge and go with what you get. We all have different ways of getting the message. Yours is a good one, trust it. Trust God and Spirit.

Yes. Spirit was definitely talking to you in New Mexico and you did receive the message.

Pictures I saw in no particular order. Spirit was guiding you away from one or more people. They were insisting you leave a place. I don't know if it was a certain landscape or moving from a place near a person. But the message was "move away from here."

You also have a strong need to fulfill this lifetime in humanitarian service. Part of your life mission is helping others, so use your intuition there as well.

Your guides will grow stronger and stronger if you will work with them regularly this year. You can make lots of progress. The universe's energy for you is about spiritual growth. Pray that God lead you there.

Peace,

Cyndy

Louisa, still in need of an answer to her ever-important mortality question, e-mailed her back and thanked her for the information. She told her that she hadn't been to New Mexico yet and needed to know if it would be a safe trip or if she should stay home.

Cyndy quickly responded and told Louisa that there was something about the land, or people associated with the land. She assured that the trip should be fine, overall, and to listen to her inner feeling.

Louisa sat quietly in thought, staring absently at her computer monitor. She saw movement on the screen and looked up in the corner and saw a new message was in her in-box. It was another e-mail from Cyndy.

"One more thing.

Exact sentence from master teacher. One I see as a purple and blue light.

Your steps toward them are being met with much delight. Keep walking forward through the fear and logic to where there is only peace and truth."

3

Malory dipped her makeup brush into the blush then quickly swiped each cheekbone, her chin, and then a dab on her nose. She pressed her lips together to spread the fresh gloss that remained there and tossed the brush into her makeup case. She glanced out the bathroom window at the dismal, afternoon sky and then up her street. No sign of Louisa yet.

She stepped over the pile of dirty clothes in the hall and went into the bedroom. She pulled her sweater over her head, stepped into her high heeled black boots and zipped them up. After one last look around the room, she walked out and shut the door behind her.

Her heels clicked on the linoleum floor as she made her way into the kitchen and she briefly noted that she carried herself with a different air of confidence when she wore them. She rinsed out her coffee cup, placed it in the sink and began to review the instructions she left for her husband, Scott. She rarely left him alone for days at a time with their seven year old daughter, but surely he could handle it. Maybe he would pick up the house while she was gone, she hoped, or make some gesture of participation.

She felt a twinge of resentment building in her chest. Alan may not have helped Louisa enough with the house or the kids, but at least he tried to celebrate her by sending her on a trip with a friend. Certainly Scott could celebrate her by running the vacuum. She wrote the check for the electric bill and placed it with the note to drop it off before the due date, then saw Louisa's car at the end of the cul-de-sac.

When Louisa pulled up in front of Malory's house, she saw her friend's tall, full figure appear in the doorway. Malory stepped out to greet her, her blonde hair falling to the middle of her back.

"You fixed up. You look really beautiful," Louisa said, stepping toward her to give her a hug. "And here I am in sweats."

"I figured I may not shower tomorrow, so what the heck," Malory said, returning the hug. "Have you been crying?" she asked, as she stepped back to look Louisa in the eyes.

"I can't think about it right now," Louisa choked, grabbing one of Malory's bags and walking to the car.

"I know honey—the boys."

"I'll be fine. I just have to let this move through me." Tears streamed down Louisa's cheeks as she helped load the overstuffed bags into the back of her tan Mazda minivan. "Mal, we're only going to be gone a couple days. What's with all the luggage?"

"What if I wish I had brought something?" Malory asked, throwing two king sized pillows into the car.

"We'd buy it for you there," Louisa said, laughing through her tears.

"You're really a mess," Malory said and used her scratchy sweater to wipe the moisture off her friend's cheek. "Crying and laughing at the same time."

"I know!" Louisa sobbed and slammed the door shut on the back of the van. "Let's just get going."

The farther they got away from town, the more the vacation spirit began to overtake Louisa's tears. After a while, she looked over at Malory and said, "I think I'm going to be okay."

"I knew you would be," said Malory turning down the radio. "Can you believe we went for almost ten years without seeing each other?"

"What on earth made you think of that?" asked Louisa, looking over at Malory in the passenger seat.

"I don't know. It just occurred to me while you were over there crying that we were so close in college and those first few years after we moved out of the dorms, and then you got all into your career and we went different directions. Now here we are going to New Mexico. Life is funny."

"It is. I'm so glad we're going. It was really nice of Alan—even though I was a little freaked out at first."

"Isn't he such a dichotomy?" Malory asked. "He can be such a chauvinist on the one hand, but he celebrates you on the other. I just don't get him."

"Neither do I." said Louisa, shaking her head. "How did you and I reconnect, anyway? I can't remember."

"You left a bag of spirituality tapes on my porch for my birthday. After all those years of not seeing each other and you reached out to me just when I needed you."

Raindrops began to patter the windshield and Louisa smiled over at Malory. "Was that when you and Scott were getting ready to separate?" she asked.

"Yeah, but I think we had gotten back together by the time you and I started having a daily narrative with each other."

"I can't imagine not having a daily narrative now," Louisa said, turning on her windshield wipers.

"Me either. I'd die without it," said Malory. She pulled out a pack of gum and handed a piece to her friend. "Are you feeling more secure about the trip?"

"I think so. Gosh, it's really raining hard now," Louisa said. Malory reached across her and turned up the wipers. "Thanks Mal. I don't know what my paranoia was about. I'd like to think I could trust my gut feeling, but my radar's off, you know. I get so overprotective of the kids."

"As it should be," said Malory. "They're still babies."

"And then I feel guilty for leaving them—for needing a break. But if I didn't take a break, I'd be less patient and I'd feel guilty about that. I guess mother's guilt gets you one way or the other."

"It does," Malory said, shaking her head. "It really does. How far should we try and make it tonight?"

"Tucumcari?"

"Tucumcari it is."

4

The next morning the New Mexico sky was a sunny, bright blue, and they passed through Santa Fe before noon. The opportunity for Louisa to sleep through the night had only opened the door of more than three years of sleep deprivation rather than leaving her rested and refreshed, so she sat with her eyes closed as Malory drove north toward Ojo Caliente. They turned off HWY 84 onto HWY 285, a smaller road that took them twisting through rocky, tree-spotted mountains.

Louisa, not quite asleep, felt a choking sensation in her throat and jolted herself awake, coughing and gasping for air. They were crossing over a bridge when she opened her eyes and there was a long mesa in front of her. Her heart began to race.

"Are you okay?" asked Malory.

"I guess I choked," Louisa said, still trying to recover. She took a drink of water and fidgeted nervously.

"What's up?" asked Malory.

"I'm feeling anxious. I hope everything's alright with the kids," Louisa said, rather than *get me the hell home*, which was what she was really thinking. She gripped the door handle as tightly as she could and took a slow, deep breath.

"I'm sure they're fine," Malory said. "Alan would call, wouldn't he?"

Louisa looked down at her cell phone. "No reception. I'm feeling that uneasiness I had a few days ago."

"I wonder what that's about?"

Louisa shrugged in response.

"Let's just agree that if either one of us feels freaked out, we'll leave."

"That sounds like a good plan," said Louisa. "But really, what could possibly happen? Everything will be fine."

Through the windshield, the vistas in every direction were wide and expansive as they wound through the rugged landscape. They finally started to see houses along the highway as they came to the small town of Ojo Caliente. They passed a convenience store with a colorful mural of Virgin Mary of Guadalupe, the Patron Saint of Mexico and its people, painted on its side and then made the turn down to the springs.

When they pulled into the unpaved parking lot, the gravel crunched beneath the tires. Getting out of the car, Louisa took in her surroundings. The backdrop was one of desert mountains and cliffs spotted with piñon and sage. To the left was a small building that led to the hot springs and to the right was the adobe hotel, its front covered by a long wooden porch. Small adobe cottages were scattered around the grounds, each resembling an old highway motel.

Once inside the hotel, Louisa saw there was no one behind the desk. The wood floor creaked as she walked over to the stucco fireplace to warm her hands. After a few minutes, a middle aged Hispanic woman emerged from a room behind the desk and greeted Louisa. "Have you been to the springs before?" she asked while she entered Louisa's information into the computer.

"No. This is my first time."

"I hope you enjoy your stay," she said. "Your room is just down the hall."

Louisa and Malory walked down the hall and found their room. The hinges on the old door squeaked as Louisa pushed it open and walked in. In the small room there were two mismatched beds, a dresser, and a turquoise vinyl chair in the corner. The bathroom had only a sink and a toilet.

"Well, the website said it was unpretentious and uncomplicated," said Malory, laughing.

"I like it," said Louisa. "It reminds me of the dorms."

"Kind of appropriate after our trip down memory lane last night, don't you think?" Malory said and started getting herself settled in.

"I'm going to go check out the springs," said Louisa. "Do you want to come?"

"No," said Malory, emptying out her bag of toiletries. "Go on without me."

"Okay. Remember, I scheduled spa packages for us and the appointment is in half an hour."

"How could I forget?" said Malory. "You're so good to me."

Louisa smiled, grabbed her swimsuit and walked out of the hotel and through the small building she had seen from the parking lot. She said "hello" to the girl behind the counter and went through a second door that led to the springs and the bath houses. The air was filled with the scent of minerals. Looking to her right, she saw a woman leaning against some rocks, sunning herself in a small pool. She walked toward the sound of a waterfall where she saw steam coming off the surface of another pool next to the cliffs.

As she made her away around the springs, she realized how little she had taken in the day she and Alan had stopped there after they were married. It had been snowing that day, so they didn't stay. Two years before that, they had been skiing in Taos and she had read about the springs and felt drawn to them. She had even planned on taking the car and driving one afternoon, but Alan had surprised her and bought her a massage. Funny, it took three tries over more than five years for her to finally get there.

A few hours later when she finished at the bath house, it was dusk. Malory was no where to be found, so Louisa determined she had gone back to the room. Walking into the cold air, she looked up at the sky and saw the orange, pink, and purple streaks as the clouds filtered the remaining sunlight. The shadowed cliffs were bluish purple, emanating a presence that grounded her. She took a deep breath and felt gratitude for being there in that moment.

When Louisa approached the door to their room, she heard a hair dryer. Malory turned and greeted her with a smile when she opened the door.

"How was your massage?" Malory asked loudly over the dryer.

"Great. I haven't had one in so long."

"A massage therapist that doesn't get massages—what's wrong with you? You know the benefits."

"It's called being a working mother of two small children," Louisa said, picking up a magazine and plopping down on one of the beds. "I did enjoy giving massages when I had the time, though."

"No. I enjoyed you giving massages when you had the time!" Malory smiled as she pulled the brush through her long blonde hair, drying the layers underneath. "Are you starving?"

Louisa nodded as she flipped through the magazine.

"You're not going to get to read that, silly. I'm already finished," Malory said, turning off the dryer. She took the magazine out of Louisa's hands and tapped her on the head. "Let's go."

Walking down the hall, Louisa ran her hand along the smooth stucco wall and admired the subtle charm of the old building. The restaurant was decorated with antique wooden tables paired with a variety of antique chairs, and the dark wood floors contrasted with the white stucco walls. Paintings and woven tapestries covered the walls, and the room glowed from the wall sconces and candles on each table. They were seated at one of the softly lit tables and gave their order to the waiter.

Malory picked up her glass of wine and looked at Louisa inquisitively from across the table. "Louisa, has your life turned out as you imagined it would when we were in college?"

Louisa sat quietly for a moment. In many ways that required some thought and she tried to remember what her perspective was back then. Career wise, she moved into her present position at twenty three after finishing her Master's degree. She wouldn't have thought that was possible, but more than that, it was the way her personal life turned out. "No," she answered. "I don't have any regrets, but back then I thought I'd end up with Matthew."

Malory nodded quietly. "What was it with you two?"

Louisa shrugged, recalling her first love that had lasted off and on for a decade. "I loved him so much, but that relationship was really hard on me."

Malory nodded again. "I remember. I always thought you two would end up together too."

Louisa shrugged and smiled. "What about you?"

"I can't really remember, but I got married a lot younger than you did."

"What made you know Scott was the one to marry?" asked Louisa.

"I just did. I knew it before we ever got together. In hindsight, I remember thinking we had these really great, connecting conversations. But you know what? Looking back, I realize that I was the one doing all the talking. So really, I was falling in love with myself."

Louisa tossed her head back and laughed. "Don't be hard on yourself. Maybe that's what we all do. When we're ready for a relationship, we see what we want to see."

"Why did you marry Alan?" asked Malory.

"Because our relationship just worked. We shared similar values and beliefs, we had fun together, and we got along great. Our main problem now is the baggage he didn't realize he carried when it came to marriage. We probably should have just kept dating." Louisa took another sip of her wine. "Dinner was great. Should we order a piece of cake for later?"

"You read my mind."

* * * *

The sky was dark when Louisa and Malory ran barefoot through patches of ice water and twenty degree temperatures toward the springs. When they made it to the pool with the small waterfall, they tossed their towels aside and quickly submerged. Louisa's toes stung from the warmth of the water, and taking a seat on the built in stone bench, she looked through the steam at the water eroded cliffs lit by a spotlight. Her eyes drifted to the night sky and she and Malory sat in silence.

There were several pools to try and they tried them all. Louisa found herself gravitating toward the iron spring that night and decided that was where she wanted to be for the remainder of the evening. She climbed down the steps and landed on the pebbly bottom. Finding a seat on the ledge, she rubbed her feet through the small stones, enjoying the heat and massage. With a deep breath, she leaned back and stared at the star-packed sky and the darkness of the cliffs against it. Within a few breaths, she felt herself being carried away…to daylight? She saw the same sky, but bright. It looked like it was maybe early afternoon. She then looked at the cliffs above her. There were Indians, three of them, looking to the east across the landscape and then down at the springs. *But wait— it's dark right now.* As quickly as her conscious awareness analyzed the experience, it ended. Louisa again saw the cliffs against a star-packed sky.

"Beautiful night," said a man stepping into the springs.

"It is," Louisa said, and once again massaged her feet with the warm stones. "It really is."

When the springs closed, Louisa returned to the room and got out of her cold bathing suit. She grabbed the piece of chocolate cake they had been saving for later and walked out to the lobby area where Malory, along with other guests in the hotel, was sitting by the fire. She climbed on the couch next to her friend, pulling her knees into her chest.

"Drink this," said Malory, handing Louisa a water bottle.

"What is it?" asked Louisa, taking a swig and making a face in disgust.

"It's water from the Lithia spring. It's supposed to remedy symptoms of depression." Louisa piled a bite of cake on the spoon and handed it to Malory.

"Maybe the combination of the chocolate and this water has elevated my serotonin levels because I'm feeling a little 'loopy,'" said Louisa.

"Well, loopy's good for you. And happy mothers are good mothers, so keep eating," Malory said, laughing and handing the bottle of Lithia water back to Louisa.

"So are you two traveling without your families?" asked a woman sitting in a chair by the fireplace.

Louisa turned and saw an older woman with long grey hair wearing linen pants, a sweater, argyle socks, and Birkenstocks.

"Yeah, a little break for the moms," answered Malory. "Her husband gave her a vacation for Christmas, so here we are."

"Wow. That's very generous of him," the woman said, "letting you be here on a vacation while he's home with the kids."

Louisa nodded her head politely. *Letting her be on vacation?* "I'm sure he's fine."

"Yeah, Alan's life *is* a vacation," said Malory, sending them both into laughter, the kind that's silent but makes your stomach hurt.

"I need to stop drinking this lithium water. It might be making me manic," said Louisa, trying to stop and catch a breath. "Or maybe it's just time to go to bed."

They said goodnight, picked up their cake and water bottle and went to the room. Louisa pulled down the covers to get into bed, and as she did, she felt a surge of energy creep up her spine. She tried to ignore it but couldn't catch her breath and felt a twinge in the pit of her stomach. She crawled under the covers and glanced at the turquoise vinyl chair next to the bed. "I don't like that chair," she said.

"What's wrong with it?" Malory asked, laughing at the silliness of the comment.

"I just don't like it. It's creeping me out." Louisa pulled the covers up to her chin.

"Maybe it's because it's empty," Malory said. She picked up her bag and put it in the chair. "Is that better?"

"No. Malory? There's a man in that corner, " Louisa said. She felt paralyzed, yet this was not a new experience for her. It was no different than the time she kept seeing a woman standing by her bed, and then had a dream one morning that the woman was a healing spirit whose name was Mary. When she told Alan about Mary, Isaac, barely two, said, "No mommy, Mary not here now. Mary bye-bye." Or the little girl in the blue jumper that stood next to Caleb's crib or next to the rocking chair when Louisa was nursing him. These things freaked Louisa out, but she was at least able to move. So what was different about this? "He's wearing gray pants and a white shirt, with suspenders."

"Well, it *is* an old place. You know, he's probably someone who worked here or something," Malory said. "Are you freaking out? Are you going to be okay?"

Louisa lay perfectly still, afraid to move. "Can I get in bed with you?"

"Of course you can. Are you going to be able to get up?" Malory asked as she pulled down the blanket on the other bed.

Mustering up the courage, Louisa threw off the covers, jumped into the bed and got as close to Malory as possible.

"Mal, I'm not myself right now."

"Yeah, I see that."

The two lay on their sides facing each other and Louisa spoke rapidly as she fired off questions. "Do you think this is what I sensed that night when I drifted off while patting Isaac to sleep? Or what the psychic meant when she said I should leave a place? Why am I so scared? Can we get out of here? Is it too late to check out?"

"I'm trying to think of what you would say to me if the tables were turned," Malory said. "I think you'd remind me that this is an old place, and it's possible he is in this space yet completely unaware of us."

Louisa rolled over onto her stomach, hugging the pillow. "Do you really expect me to acknowledge my beliefs about space and time right now? I mean *really*. That requires rationality. Do I seem rational right now?"

"Well, at least you have your sense of humor," Malory said with a smile. "This has happened to you before, so why is this bothering you so much?"

"It feels different, that's all."

Louisa rolled back onto her side and closed her eyes, reaching the acceptance they would be staying the night. Even with her eyes closed, she could feel the presence in the room. A few more moments passed, and she felt a shift— a peaceful feeling wrapped itself around her like a blanket as she became aware of something to her left. It was another male figure. He was an Indian. He was wearing brown hide pants, no shirt, and had something around his neck. His dark hair hung loose about his shoulders and he held a spear or stick next to him. Louisa put her hand on Malory's arm and whispered what she saw.

"Why are you whispering?" Malory asked in a hushed tone. "If it's a ghost, he'll still be able to hear you."

"Malory!"

"Well, it's true! You don't seem as scared right now though," she said.

"I'm not. Mal?"

"Huh?"

"His name is Running Bear."

Malory burst into laughter. "Oh my God—don't you see there is something going on here?"

"Sort of," Louisa said, closing her eyes to go to sleep. "I thought I liked this place, but maybe I don't. It's making me question my sanity."

Malory chuckled beside her, and with a deep breath, Louisa let her head relax into the pillow and fell asleep.

She sat next to Malory by the Cliffside spring. In her lap she held a photo album. She flipped through the pages of black and white photographs and pointed different pictures out to Malory. With the turn of each page, she felt herself slip further and further away from Malory and back in time, until she was surrounded by darkness. Fading into view was a pale grid- work of light. As she moved farther into the grid-work, she felt herself disappearing into it. She was filled with a peaceful sense of home and the small part she played in the grid. Then, in an instant, she spiraled back toward her body.

When Louisa opened her eyes, the pale morning light lit the small room. She recalled the dream she had upon waking and felt the last remains of the grid of light and how peaceful it felt. She looked over at Malory whose eyes were still closed. Malory had cracked the window the night before and the cold January air shocked Louisa as she kicked off the covers. Shutting the window, she quickly jumped back into the warm bed.

"Yeah, it's a little cold," Malory said with her eyes still closed.

"Feel my face. It's like I have been hanging in a meat locker," said Louisa.

Malory reached her hand over, touched Louisa's cheek and giggled.

"Did I wake you up?" asked Louisa.

"No. But I'm glad you got up to close that window so I didn't have to," Malory said. "How'd you do last night?"

"Well, I'm amazed, but I survived," said Louisa.

"Good. So, is the gang still here?"

"They appear to be, yes. I think I'll ignore them."

"Good plan. I'm starving. What time is it?"

Louisa looked at the clock. "Seven. The restaurant doesn't open for a half hour. How about we bundle up and go for a walk?"

Malory agreed, so the two women got dressed and went out to greet the morning. They walked in silence, watching the sun rise behind the mountains. A part of Louisa wanted to talk about what happened the night before, but she didn't want to make more of it than it was. When they made it to the top of the hill that led to the main highway, they both stopped and stared at the eastern sky. Louisa closed her eyes and took a deep breath of cold air, letting it out slowly. When she opened her eyes, she and Malory turned to look at each other in unison and smiled. With a mutual nod, they turned back for the hotel.

The lobby was warm, with a fire burning in the stucco fireplace. Louisa immediately walked over and sat next to it, pulling off her scarf and gloves. Malory settled in on the couch with a cup of coffee from the courtesy pot and started to flip through a magazine.

After a few minutes when her back was as hot as she could tolerate, Louisa stood up and looked to her left. Had she not noticed the small room adjacent to the lobby the night before? There was a TV in the corner and chairs along the wall. On the wall opposite the chairs were some old black and white photos. She strolled over to take a look and could see they were taken some time ago. One of the photos was of a group of people—probably a family. Scanning their faces, her heart stopped when she looked at the man standing beside the others. "Hey Mal, come look at this."

Putting down her coffee, Malory came over and looked at the picture and at the man Louisa was pointing to. "Is that him?"

Louisa nodded.

"He has 'Poppy' written underneath him. This must be his family. See, I told you last night he was probably tied to this place." Malory clapped her hands together. "This is so cool," she said excitedly. "Come on. The restaurant just opened."

Louisa looked at the picture one last time. A lump formed in her throat as she studied his eyes. She put her hand on her chest and took a deep breath, confused by the strong response he evoked in her, then followed Malory into the restaurant.

On the drive home the next day, Malory asked her how she felt about the things that occurred on the trip. All Louisa could say was that she felt confused. But in spite of her fears, both before she left and after arriving in Ojo, Louisa made it home safely. Walking in the door, she was greeted by her boys and thrust into the chaos of home life. No transition, no few minutes to unwind like Alan was allowed when he got home from work; just an immediate inundation of parenting and wifely responsibilities. It was life as usual, as if she had never been gone. It wasn't until she got the kids fed, bathed, and in bed that she excitedly told Alan what had happened on the trip.

As Louisa shared her story and looked back on the events that led her to Ojo, she began to sense that the groundwork was being laid for a journey beyond her imagining. Little did Louisa know then that Alan was intuitively guiding her where she needed to be or that Malory was the perfect person to accompany her. Even her odd feelings that something was going to happen were accurate and she would come to learn how prophetic the e-mail from the psychic actually was.

5

She surveys her surroundings. She's back at Ojo Caliente. The people with her are familiar, but she doesn't know them in her waking state. They are having some kind of a meeting. "Am I dreaming?" She intuitively knows this is Ojo, but it doesn't look like the landscape she saw when she was there. And who are these people?

Then, within whatever place she is visiting, she falls into another dream and finds herself in another body. She is female and running; running as if for her life. She can see her dark feet and can feel the rocks beneath them as she skillfully navigates the rough terrain. She is running south, along a river. The afternoon sun is shining through the trees as the flimsy leaves flutter in the wind. "I don't remember trees like these at Ojo," she thinks within her dream. She keeps running, breathing hard, the strangled sound of her voice intermingling with each exhale.

He reaches out and skims her sleeve with his hand. She pushes ahead, harder, but he has caught up with her. Suddenly, she is being held under the cold water. She can feel his strong hands holding her shoulder and head beneath the surface. She can feel the water rushing across her face as she thrashes to get free of his hold, struggling for a chance to breathe. Her resolve begins to weaken and she feels herself surrender. She hears the words that belong to this woman who is her, yet not Louisa. "You think you can harm me, but you can't." And in that instant, her spirit spirals out of her body as if traveling through the point of a cone.

She then finds herself back in the location of the first dream. She calls out to Malory, and instantly she is before her. "This is what happened..." Louisa says, and tells Malory of the girl's experience.

"That's exactly what happened," Malory says emphatically.

Louisa woke up with a jolt. It was a dream. Caleb had cried out, hadn't he? No, he was right next to her sleeping soundly. Her chest felt tight, so she reached in the drawer for the old inhaler. As she rolled over to go back to sleep, she was hit with the impact of the bizarre dream and replayed what she could remember in her mind. *I think I better write this down.* She turned on the light and reached for a piece of paper and purple crayon Isaac had left on the night table.

* * * *

It had been over a month since her trip to New Mexico, and distracted by the responsibilities of daily life, Louisa had tucked Ojo away as memory. But her dream life had been anything but ordinary, and on the way to work the morning after her dream about the drowning, she called Malory and told her about it.

"There's something to it, Mal."

"After what happened on the trip, I'd say I agree. Tell me, have you had any other weird dreams?"

"Actually," Louisa said as she slowed down to turn toward the office, "I have had several in which a guy I went to high school with is trying to tell me something. Over and over again in my dreams he has said 'I need to tell you where you are,' or 'let me tell you where you are,' but I could never remember what he told me. Once he left me a book, but when I tried to read it, it was written in symbols, and once he gave me a video, but I couldn't find a VCR. Then I woke up not too long ago and remembered he said I was in 'theta.'"

"Interesting," said Malory. "Is 'theta' some kind of a wave? Like alpha waves in meditation?"

"I'm not sure," said Louisa.

"I'm walking to my computer right now," Malory said. "Okay, I'm doing the search. Are you at the office yet?"

"I'm turning into the parking lot."

"Oh my god, listen to this," said Malory. "This is in regard to different brain waves. It says that 'in alpha, 7-12 hertz, we begin to access the wealth of creativity that lies just below our conscious awareness. It is the gateway, or entry point, into deeper states of consciousness.' It then lists theta waves, 4-7hz. 'Theta is one of the more elusive and extraordinary realms we can explore. It is also known as the twilight state which we normally only experience fleetingly when we arise out of the depths of delta (deep sleep) or drifting off to sleep. In theta, we are in a waking dream. Vivid imagery flashes before the mind's eye and we are receptive to information beyond our normal conscious awareness.' Interesting. This website is talking about 'theta' in the context of the shamanic state of consciousness. There you have it. You're a shaman disguised as a stressed out mother of two toddlers."

"Maybe so," Louisa said with a laugh. "You got the 'stressed out' part right."

"That's pretty cool," said Malory. "Something's brewing with you and you need to be writing it down."

Later that night, Louisa sat at the desk in the study and pulled out a blank journal that had been sitting in the drawer for more than a year. She found a pen and began to write about her trip to New Mexico, Poppy, and her dreams upon returning.

* * * *

Journal Entry

February 23

My dream about the female who was drowned was so vivid and real. I could feel the water as it rushed past me, my hair in my face, his hands holding me under. I also can't deny it's a bit odd to have repeated dreams about someone trying to tell me I am in a "theta" state. Are my dreams trying to tell me I am visiting that state, thus able to access things I can't access otherwise? Whatever is going on with me has caught my attention and I am recalling the seeker once in me that has all but been forgotten.

It's unclear in my memory when the mystical experiences started for me, but in adolescence they ignited my curiosity and I found myself over the course of several years immersed in studying not only the history of Christianity and the other major religions, but what had come to be known as "new age" writings as well. As a result, I came to hold new conclusions and perspectives on the soul, physical life, and consciousness.

As a college student who took many of the basic courses in the Social Sciences, I had a lot of information in my memory bank about the subject of "consciousness": what it was, how it could be divided, how it operated, and lots of other Freudian or neo-Freudian theory. While each theorist had something beneficial to contribute, psychology seemed to stop short to me. I now understand that I believe consciousness is far more than traditional psychology considers it to be. Defined as "the state of being aware, able to feel and think, or aware of one's self as a thinking being," it is implied that we have consciousness because we are physically alive. How, then, does one go about categorizing mystical experiences if it is implied that consciousness exists as a result of physical matter? The only logical conclusion for me is that consciousness precedes matter, not the other way around.

When Malory and I left Ojo, it felt as if a door within me had been cracked open, but the world hasn't moved beneath my feet and my life has carried on with its normal rhythm. Yet the timing of this personal experience can only be described as serendipitous. Just when I was struggling to balance being a wife, mother and career woman, and how to find contentedness when my life was centered on the needs of everyone else, I was handed nothing short of a mystery—and one that belongs to only me. And while it would be nice to understand why Ojo affected me the way it did, for now I will simply accept it as one of those rare and wonderful occurrences that demonstrate there is far more to our existence than we will ever know. But I do know one thing: I want go back to Ojo Caliente.

6

She's in her house. There is a baby in the sling she carried Caleb in, but wrapped more tightly like a papoose, hanging on the back of the door as she swept the floor. She doesn't know the baby's full name, but knows that "Silva" is part of it.

She discovers baby "Silva" is gone. She's panicked, looking all over for him. Then it hits her: someone took her baby. She tries to get her computer on-line to do some research, like this would be the way she could find him, but she can't get her computer to respond.

She then realizes that the baby was given to the father's brother. It isn't Alan's brother, because this baby isn't Alan's. Whoever the father is, he gave her baby to his brother and she had to get him back.

Louisa slowly opened her eyes. *What a vivid and bizarre dream.* She got out of bed and walked into Caleb's room. The room was filled with the dim glow of the nightlight and Caleb was curled up holding the handle on his red and blue pacifier. She then peeked in on Isaac, who was sprawled across his bed with his head hanging off the mattress. She rotated him so his head rested on his Scooby pillow and went back to bed.

* * * *

A year had passed and another Christmas had come and gone. Louisa held herself in downward dog as the yoga video instructed and then moved to a lunge position. She looked up and saw the Christmas tree still aglow though it was well into January. Back into downward dog she went and she felt the stretch in her calves as she pressed her heels to the floor. She must have made the unconscious decision to keep the tree up until the Epiphany, or had it already passed? She moved to lunge position on the other leg and looked at the tree again, admiring the orange and amber lights she had used in the spirit of trying something different. She should probably take it down before leaving for Ojo, which would be in two days.

When Alan had asked her what she wanted for Christmas, she asked for the freedom to go back to New Mexico with Malory. In that way, she and Malory would both be getting a gift from Alan, though she wondered if he would give her his credit card like he did last time or if the freedom to go itself was the actual gift. After being together for six years, they still hadn't combined checking accounts, nor did they share a credit card. The only problem with this was that she felt, after paying the bills that came out of her account, that she still lived paycheck to paycheck on her social work salary. Alan was a financial advisor making four times what she did, yet her psychology about financial affairs was the same as when she was single, meaning one of scarcity. Alan had once somewhat jokingly told her that his money was his money and her money was his money, but it must not have bothered her much since she never pushed for a joint account—or maybe she had been single so long she felt like she had to give every last dime to do her financial share. Regardless, Santa came through for her on the Ojo trip, and she was going no matter where the funding for it came from.

She ended on the floor in child's pose and stayed there until the credits on the video were well finished. She turned off the TV and the lights, except for the Christmas tree which now cast its amber glow across the living room, and walked back to the bedrooms. Isaac's door was only open a crack and when she tried to push it open, it wouldn't budge. She peered in and saw that Alan was lying against the door, and both he and Isaac were asleep on the floor. She had asked Alan to put Isaac to bed since he hadn't in almost a year and it was important the kids didn't feel completely thrown from their routine while she was gone. It hadn't gone well, but she told him to figure out how to deal with it. Apparently his only way of keeping Isaac from walking out of the room was to barricade the door with his body. She didn't bother to try and wake him and went on to bed herself. She fell asleep quickly and found herself in a lucid dream.

She looks in the distance and sees a large, old barn. There are massive trees to the left of it and smaller ones to the right. The barn has been renovated and turned into a Bed & Breakfast. She knows she is back in Ojo Caliente, but none of this looks familiar.

She and Malory are in the B & B. She feels a strong sense of familiarity. Remembering something, she turns to Malory and asks, "What's to the west of here? I know there is a place to the west of here," she says. "Isn't this where I slept in a hammock?"

Instantly, she finds herself in another body. She swings her legs out of the hammock and places her feet on the cold, dirt floor. "Whose feet are these?" she asks herself. Suddenly, she is back with Malory before her. "Yes! That's where I slept in a hammock," she says, again pointing to the west.

Louisa heard barking and it pulled her out of her dream. There must have been a deer in the yard again. She hoped Alan would take care of it but after she lay in bed a few more minutes, the dogs continued to bark. *No such luck.* The house was cold when she pulled back the covers. When she flipped on the porch light, she saw snow had fallen and she hurried the dogs out the back door.

As she got back into bed, she recalled her dream. *Where did I sleep in the hammock?* For the life of her, she couldn't remember, but it was *so* familiar. She lay awake for another fifteen minutes, searching her memory for when she slept in the hammock. It was just within her grasp, but not quite.

Two days later, a CD of 70's music was in the player as Louisa and Malory pulled into Tucumcari, New Mexico to sleep for the night. Andy Gibb was wailing out "I Just Want to be Your Everything."

"If you give a little more than you're asking for your love will turn the key," they sang in unison, then looked at each other knowingly and

laughed. It was so simple. They, the husbands, just didn't get it. Give a little more than you're asking for; the key to a successful relationship — right there in an Andy Gibb song.

"I need to play this for a certain someone," Malory said.

"Amen," said Louisa. "But hey, 2003 is going to be a great year. How could it not be when we're on a vacation at the very beginning of it?"

They checked into a hotel and had lights out by eleven. The room was dark except for the light from outside that made a frame around the heavy curtains and Louisa lay awake for what seemed like an eternity. She felt anxious and wanted to talk to Malory, but the soft snore from the next bed indicated Malory was already asleep. She slowly began to relax.

She is in another body. She looks down from a high point of a mesa and sees the landscape is clearly of the southwest. She sees what looks like an army setting up camp. Her heart begins to beat rapidly. She then finds herself in another dream, running along the river. "Oh, it's the drowning dream again," she says to herself. She pushes ahead as fast as she can but he grabs her sleeve-

Louisa jerked herself up in bed, her tank top damp with sweat. She looked at the clock and saw it was somehow four o'clock in the morning, though it felt like she had just fallen asleep. Malory heard her stirring and turned on the light.

"Did you have a bad dream?" asked Malory, squinting and rubbing her eyes.

"I think I was about to have the drowning dream again," said Louisa. "Remember the one from last year? But this time there was some sort of army. Why are you awake?"

"I don't know. Maybe to talk to you about your recurring dream," said Malory. "Have you had any other dreams lately?"

Louisa sat up to face the bed that Malory was in. Sitting cross legged, she pulled the covers up around her shoulders and told Malory about baby "Silva" and how he was taken from her. "Do you think my dream is trying to tell me if I get pregnant, something is going to happen to the baby?"

"Where does that stand, anyway? Is Alan opening up to the idea of having another one?" asked Malory.

"He seems to be softening," said Louisa. "If it means sex, I can probably persuade him."

"And you do all the work after that, so hey, it shouldn't be a problem," Malory said sarcastically as she propped herself up on her mound of pillows. "Okay, let's get back to the dream. If the baby wasn't Alan's, I'd say if you were trying to tell yourself something, it wasn't that. Have you had any other dreams?"

"I had the dream about the baby about a week ago and then the other night I had a really vivid dream about us being back at Ojo," said Louisa. She shared her dream about the barn and how she found herself in another body sleeping in the hammock. "I laid there for the longest time trying to remember when I slept in a hammock, it felt so familiar."

"I can't believe you had that dream and didn't tell me," Malory said in a flat yet shocked tone. Louisa shrugged and pulled a pillow into her lap.

Malory rolled onto her side to face Louisa. "It's a bit odd, these dreams where you're in someone else's body," Malory said. "That sounds Mexican— the sleeping in hammocks. We haven't talked about any of this since last winter, but maybe you need to look at this in context of what happened last time we were here."

Louisa nodded with some hesitancy then spoke. "Malory, I feel like I've been there before. That's why I was so freaked out last year and why I'm experiencing events from someone else's viewpoint— because they *are* from someone else's perspective."

"Reincarnation," said Malory.

Louisa nodded.

"I think we can agree that that's a given."

A given? And why was it happening? As intriguing as it all was, Louisa began to wonder if she really wanted to know.

7

From where she stood catching her breath, Louisa could look down and see the old hotel, the cottages, and the minivan in the parking lot. After being in the car all morning she felt like she needed to get her blood flowing, so when they arrived in Ojo, she had sprinted up the steep trail. Her white, long sleeve t-shirt was damp with sweat and the cold January breeze gave her goose bumps.

They had left the hotel early and Louisa had been filled with anticipation as the morning sun revealed the vast New Mexico landscape that was covered in a blanket of darkness when they had pulled off the highway the night before. Because they arrived early they weren't able to check into the small house where they were going to stay, so Louisa went into the office to get a map of trails in the area. The trail she took led to somewhere called "Posi," and she decided to check it out. Malory declined the hiking offer and was somewhere sitting and having a smoke.

Louisa sat on a rock at the top of the steep portion of trailhead that led to Posi. She faced south, but could see mountains and mesas scattered in every direction. In her direct line of vision was a long, tree covered mesa which she studied with great thought. When they had turned off the highway outside of Española to head toward the springs, she had what could only be described as an anxiety attack and her breathing was suddenly strained. They had just passed over a bridge, and when she looked up, there was a massive mesa in front of them. She had recalled the year before when she felt adamant that she wanted to go home. Was the mesa she was now studying the same land mass? The anxiety, the dreams— it was almost as if the drama that started a year earlier had picked right up where it left off.

A tingling ran up Louisa's spine and she felt a presence behind her right shoulder. She could see a woman in her mind's eye—it was the woman in the hammock, as if they were separated by nothing more than a thin veil. She tried to swallow but felt a lump in her throat. The woman's presence calibrated into Louisa's, familiar while still unknown. Instead of panicking, Louisa spoke to her silently. "Yes, I see you," she said, and then to distract herself, she pulled from her pocket the trail map and some brochures she had picked up in the lobby. The breeze was strong, and she placed all but the map underneath her thigh to keep things from blowing away. As she studied the map, she saw there was a river labeled "Rio Ojo." Was that the river she dreamed about when she was in another body? She closed her eyes and listened to the silence for a few more seconds, then turned to hike down and find Malory.

At the bottom of the trail, she scanned the area until she saw Malory sitting on a bench next to a small labyrinth made of rocks. "Mal, look at this," she called as she approached her, out of breath. "There's a river that runs through this area."

"You drove over it to get here. Where were you?" Malory asked sarcastically.

"I did?"

"This place messes you up," Malory said, taking the map then looking at Louisa questioningly. "The woman who was drowned?"

"You read my mind."

Malory stood and pushed up the sleeves on her sweatshirt. "Let's go."

The two crossed the parking lot and made their way through thick brush and trees to the river's edge. The water rushed past them and Louisa knelt down to put her hand into its cold current. She stared at the water in silence until she felt something pulling her. "We need to go that way," she said, pointing north.

"North it is," Malory said, asking no questions. As they walked purposefully to the car, Malory tossed the keys to Louisa and they got in.

Louisa's heart pounded as she drove to the main highway, so she softly sang along with Gordon Lightfoot playing in the CD player. She drove north until she saw the first road that would take them toward the river. They wound through the mountains for no more than a few minutes when Louisa felt the sudden urge to pull off onto the narrow shoulder.

"Here?" Malory asked.

Louisa nodded and turned off the ignition.

"Let's get our bearings so we know what to look for in case we get lost," Malory said.

"There's a sign for a school down the road. Will that work?" asked Louisa.

"Sounds good," said Malory. "Are you ready?"

"For what, I'm not sure. But I'm ready."

They trekked down the steep hill that led to the river. The landscape was dramatically different than what Louisa had seen at Ojo during their first trip. There were tall trees along the water line. She closed her eyes and recalled the leaves on the trees along the river in her dream, and the way the sunlight made them shimmer. They were cottonwoods, as were these.

They charged ahead for several minutes until Louisa finally stopped. "I don't know where I'm taking us."

"My gut tells me you're close to *something*, though I have no idea what," said Malory. "You were pretty decisive that this is where we needed to be. We could use a machete to cut through this brush, though. Look at this huge scratch on my neck."

Louisa examined the long, bloody mark on Malory's neck. "I'm sorry. Let's head back to the car," said Louisa, turning to climb back up the hill. "I don't know what I'm trying to find. Besides, my chest is tight again."

"Do you have your inhaler?" asked Malory.

"I forgot it," Louisa called from her position in front of Malory as they backtracked through the brush.

"Every time you have dreams about this place you need it, and you forgot it?"

"That's only happened a few times."

"Whatever! Someone drowned 'you' around here and she makes you have trouble breathing!"

"I'll will it away," Louisa said, wheezing.

A few minutes later, they reached the top of the steep hill that had led them down to the river. Malory bent down with her hands on her knees, catching her breath. "I'm not in good enough shape for this terrain." Louisa chuckled in response and pulled thorny plant debris out of her socks, then leaned against the car looking down over the river and the small mountains on the other side.

"So what do you think is north of here that was pulling you?" Malory asked, looking over at Louisa.

"I have no idea. If I didn't consider myself normal, I'd say it was borderline insanity." Louisa paused for a few moments. "But I don't think this is where the woman drowned. It's something else, but not that. Does that sound crazy?"

"No, but sometimes we share a brain, so it may not mean much," said Malory, now leaning against the car next to Louisa. She used her hand as a visor against the afternoon sun and surveyed her surroundings.

"It means a lot. That's why you're the person here with me," said Louisa.

Malory smiled at Louisa and nodded. "That's what friends are for."

"I hope friends are for sharing a bed, because I may be sleeping with you tonight."

"Of course," said Malory. "But for now I think a soak in the springs and a massage should keep you distracted for a while. Sound good?"

"Sounds perfect."

8

Malory placed the screen in front of the fire, picked up her morning coffee and sat down with a magazine. She absent mindedly flipped through the pages, then set it in her lap and stared out the window. After their hike along the river the day before, they had spent the remainder of the afternoon and evening in the warm water and at the spa. She was already relaxed and rejuvenated, as if she'd been on vacation a week.

Louisa was still in bed, which was out of character, and Malory wondered how long it had taken her to settle down and fall asleep the night before. It was clear to her that this location deeply affected Louisa. She recalled watching her during their first trip a year ago as she climbed some rocks on the hillside and thinking she looked like a gazelle, as if it was second nature for her to navigate the landscape. As she watched her that day, for a brief moment she saw Louisa as someone else; another female who was indigenous to the area. Maybe that was why she agreed so easily that Louisa had "been" in this location before.

Reincarnation was something she accepted wholeheartedly. She and Louisa had found in one another someone who spoke the same spiritual language early on in their friendship, which was quite a gift. There were times over the fifteen years of their friendship when she felt out of touch with that part of herself, and a phone call to Louisa would help her reengage with Spirit. Louisa always said it did the same thing for her.

Malory ran her finger across the scratch on her neck from their trek along the river the day before. She knew that Louisa was pulled there for a reason, but what could it be? And why was Louisa fearful of Ojo in spite of her love for it?

Malory knew her friend well—all of Louisa's issues were an open book. Abandonment was the big one, and that meant both physically and emotionally, and Louisa would tell you those were the feelings she remembers most strongly from childhood. If only Alan understood that emotional abandonment was just as valid as not showing up, Malory imagined he and Louisa would have a great marriage. Hell, what was she talking about? It was a root issue for her as well, which was one of the reasons she could turn to Louisa when she felt her most vulnerable— she understood the depths to which she could feel alone. *If you give a little more than you're asking for, the love will turn the key.* If friends give that so easily, why don't husbands? But she was digressing from her original stream of thought, which was Louisa's baggage, not hers.

So if Louisa had a connection with Ojo, perhaps her fear and uneasiness were because it brought up her emotional weaknesses. But obviously she was open to this experience or she wouldn't be having it, right? Yet it seemed like Louisa, *living it*, was taking it one step at a time as if she didn't see the potential magnitude the way Malory, from the outside, could see it. Other lifetimes, reaching out to you across the space time continuum? That could be big stuff.

Louisa sat up in bed and looked at the clock. She slipped out from beneath the warm covers and pulled on a pair of sweatpants and then her sweatshirt. She opened the bedroom door and made her way into the living room.

"Hey sleepy head," said Malory.

"I was so relieved to see sunlight filling the room when I opened my eyes," said Louisa as she climbed over the arm rest of the couch and took a seat.

"I noticed you got back in your own bed," said Malory. "What time did you finally fall asleep?"

"I think I dozed off and on because I had lots of dreams, but I think it was almost four."

"Any you remember?"

Louisa reached down for her tennis shoes. "Yeah, I had one about a house. The walls were painted pink which really stuck with me and someone gave me a dress. It felt like an Ojo dream, but it didn't make much sense. Houses aren't generally pink." She picked up the brochures she had thrown on the table the day before along with the map. In one she had read there were two tribes, the Tewa and the Tiwa Indians, that lived in the Ojo basin along the Chama river; the Chama feeds the Rio Ojo. These springs were a sacred site for the tribes. "I think I'm going to follow that trail up the mountainside that I started yesterday. There's a site of some kind at the top. Do you want to come?"

"No. Get some exercise for me too," said Malory.

Louisa tossed the brochures on the table, wrapped her scarf around her neck and put on her gloves.

"That's a great look sweetie," teased Malory. "Those same old blue sweatpants and sweatshirt you've been wearing for two days. The scarf and gloves really add a nice touch."

"Thank you. I think I wore these same clothes the entire trip last year."

"And unless you decide to wear something different, you'll be two for two," Malory said, smiling.

"Consider it part of my charm," Louisa said as she tossed the end of her scarf over her shoulder for dramatic flair. "Enjoy your peace and quiet. If you want to, we can go eat when I get back."

Louisa grabbed a water bottle and walked into the morning sun. It was a bright, clear day, and the juxtaposition of the cliffs against the blue sky was striking. She took a deep breath of cold air and walked toward the trailhead.

She made her way up the first section of trail she had climbed the day before, but it felt steeper first thing in the morning and the front of her thighs felt weak by the time she reached the top. She sat down on a big rock and took in the expansiveness of her surroundings as she caught her breath. She looked to the southeast at the long dark mesa in the distance, the mountains around Taos, and for a moment wished Alan was there to see it.

After catching her breath, she started down the trail. The steepness had leveled off to an easy grade and she walked past evergreens and cacti. They seemed so small, as did she, surrounded by the large rock formations and mountains that spanned in every direction. Aside from the breeze there was complete silence and she found herself slipping into a moving meditative state.

A subtle shift began and in the forefront of her mind was the vision she had her first trip to Ojo when sitting in the Iron spring; the vision in bright daylight of the Indians looking down on the springs. Her mind then turned to the brochure—the Tewa and the Tiwa that had lived there, and the springs that were sacred to them. She felt uneasiness wash over her. As uneasiness turned into inexplicable fear, she turned and hiked back to the springs.

When Louisa walked in the door, Malory was sitting in the same orange vinyl chair as when she left. She put down her magazine and reached for one of the brochures. "Had you read all of these?" she asked.

"Not yet, why?" said Louisa, slipping off her shoes.

"You're going to want to sit down for this," said Malory, moving to sit next to Louisa on the couch. "Remember Poppy? You want to know what his name was?"

"What was it?"

"His name was Antonio Silva and he was the one who started this place. *Silva,*" Malory said with great emphasis. Louisa repeated the words over in her mind. *Silva?*

"Are you thinkin' what I'm thinkin'?" Malory said excitedly. "Are you putting the pieces together?"

"Silva was the name of the baby in my dream who was taken and given to the father's brother?" Louisa tried to process the swirling in her mind. Was it just a coincidence that the name "Silva" so vividly came to her in a dream not a week before coming to Ojo? She sat back and hugged her knees. "What time period are we talking about?"

"This place was started around 1880."

Louisa's thoughts turned to the female who had been haunting her since the day before. "Was the woman in the hammock somehow related to Silva? Did he take her baby? Was she someone who had a relationship with him that resulted in a child? I wonder what the connection is and if I'll ever find out."

"You got a name in the dream state, Louisa. That is so cool."

"Or a coincidence."

"I know you know better than that," Malory said, leaning forward and smiling at her. "Ready for breakfast?"

"I'm starving."

Malory went back to the bedroom and threw on her jeans and a red hooded sweatshirt, the same one she had been wearing since they left, and the two walked over to the old hotel.

The old floor creaked its welcome as they walked into the lobby and Malory went to the doorway of the restaurant, but Louisa walked past the fireplace into the small room adjacent to the lobby where she had seen the picture of Poppy the year before. She knew more now than she did then— his name was Antonio Silva, and she suspected that she, as another woman, had lived there before. While she had told Malory it may all have been a coincidence, deep down she knew it wasn't. She felt she knew Silva, or the energy of his character, as well as the woman behind the veil. But her heart sank when she saw a barren wall.

Louisa walked over to the desk. "Excuse me. There were some black and white photographs on the wall when we were here last year. Have they been moved?"

"There are new owners of the springs, so someone came and took them," said the woman.

"Do you know where they are?" asked Louisa.

The woman shrugged and shook her head. "I'm sorry."

Louisa, filled with disappointment, smiled and thanked her, then went to find Malory in the restaurant.

The smell of coffee and sausage filled the air and bright paintings by a local artist adorned the walls. Louisa took a seat next to Malory. She examined the paintings as she held her mug of tea, waiting for her oatmeal while Malory read a magazine that was left on the table next to theirs. As they sat in silence, Louisa felt a tingling sensation move up her spine, causing her to sit up straight in her chair.

"What's up?" Malory asked.

"She's here, the woman in the hammock. I can feel her," Louisa said, looking over her right shoulder. She closed her eyes and heard an inner voice. When she opened them she looked at Malory. "Her name sounds like 'Martina'."

Malory looked at Louisa with raised eyebrows and volunteered, "Maria? That's a Spanish name."

"No. It sounds like 'Martina.' With a 't.' I wish I knew who she was," Louisa said, just as their food arrived. She sprinkled some brown sugar and raisins in her oatmeal while Malory made a sandwich out of her egg, sausage, and pancake. "Malory, do you feel her too?"

"No. But I believe you. If she's part of your gestalt, I might not feel her the way you do."

"Yes. She's part of my gestalt" said Louisa, contemplating Malory's words. "That's a good way to put it. If she's part of my gestalt, then the answers are inside me, right?"

"I imagine so."

"But I might need your internet skills."

"You're going to try and find her," Malory said, sitting back and smiling.

Louisa smiled.

Adelina

9

She sat on the step of the wooden porch, her long brown skirt resting on the ground. Her dark hair hung loose and the white of her sleeveless undergarment glowed against the increasing darkness. The first stars were coming into view and the cool air nipped at the skin on her bare arms and shoulders. She wrapped her shawl more tightly to fend off the chill. She could hear the river in the distance as it made its way over the rocks, and the peaks of mountains at Rancho de Taos reflected the pink of the last sunlight. She should have felt happy, but instead she already felt her impending loneliness.

The door opened behind her and the porch creaked as Antonio stepped out and knelt behind her, kissing her neck.

"I must go."

Adelina stood to look at him. His dark hair contrasted with the white of his shirt, still open and un-tucked. He gave her a gentle kiss and put on the jacket he had draped over the railing of the porch.

"I don't want you to go," she said, looking down at their feet, his in black boots, hers bare.

"I know, but I must." He stroked her hair, kissed her forehead and left her standing on the porch as he always did.

"When will I see you again?" she called, desperate to keep him talking to her so he wouldn't leave.

"Soon. I promise you will see me very soon." He untied his horse from the tree, climbed on and was quickly out of her sight. She listened until she could no longer hear the sound of hooves stomping the packed, dirt path that led back to the plaza.

Adelina had lived here, in Ojo Caliente, since she was eight years old when she left home to work as a servant to the Silva family. Her wages, at least for a time, were sent back home. She was part of a bargain between her father and Antonio, and as she grew older, she came to learn that at one time her family controlled a good deal of the land in northern New Mexico through the land grant. As customary under Spanish law, her Uncle had parceled sections of the land to other Hispano farmers and each land owner within the grant shared ownership of the common lands, which made up the majority of the grant.

A group of white men, referred to as "The Santa Fe Ring," swindled the Hispano villagers out of their farms by telling them if they signed over their deeds they would be given money, but they could stay and farm the land for the rest of their lives. Not knowing better, the villagers agreed, and inadvertently gave up ownership of the common lands as well. The "Ring" was then in control of the majority of the land and sold it to the railroad for a great profit.

Antonio was a member of the "Ring" as well. His business interests were the hot springs which lay on the common lands under the Ojo Caliente land grant and, with the help of Adelina's father, he swindled the farmers there too. The rumor was that her father provided this service to the "Ring" for two dollars of gold and a few barrels of whisky. Was he paid extra for her? She would never know, but what she did know was that she hated her father for making her leave her home; almost as much as the locals in Ojo Caliente hated Antonio.

Adelina walked back into the small adobe house and stoked the fire Antonio had made before he left. This was where she and Antonio met, but she lived in the servant's quarters of his home where she had lived for seven years. At fifteen she had been his mistress for more than a year but she believed him when he spoke of his love for her because she loved him deeply too.

She curled up in the hammock that would be her bed. The flames of the fire danced, casting moving shadows on the earthen walls. She let herself dream of the time when she could be Antonio's wife, then startled herself out of the daydream when a face flashed in her mind. It was Libby, Antonio's wife. Adelina's contentedness was rapidly replaced with feelings of jealousy and betrayal. Antonio said that his marriage was a part of an "east coast business arrangement," but it was still Libby he went home to.

She closed her eyes and sought the comfort in his words to her as they parted. "Soon. I promise you will see me very soon."

Louisa
10

Louisa slowly rocked in time with the lullaby playing on the light-up music box attached to the side of the crib. Caleb had his head on her shoulder and watched the lights as he sucked on his pacifier. She and Malory had left New Mexico at dawn that morning and she rested her tired eyes while she rubbed Caleb's back in small circular motions. When his breathing began to slow, she lifted him into his crib. "Lie down sweetie," she said, patting his back a while longer. "Close your eyes and go night-night."

She then stepped into Isaac's room where he sat on top of his pillow, still awake.

"Hey baby. Lie down and I'll pat your back," she whispered.

"Mommy, I love you past the space planet," he said.

"Oh, I love you farther than that," she said, kissing him on the forehead. She lay down next to him and pulled his blanket over his shoulders. Within minutes his breathing slowed, his eyes closed, and he slipped into sleep.

Louisa went into the living room to find Alan asleep on the couch. Walking past him, she went to the kitchen to start the dishwasher, got a glass of water and made her way back to the computer.

"Okay, let's see what we can find." She would start with Antonio Silva since his was the only name she had. Going to Google, she typed his name and clicked "search." "There you are," she said with surprise, and went on to read an excerpt from the Political Graveyard.

Silva, Antonio, a delegate from the Territory of New Mexico; born in Taos N. Mex., 1848; attended Lux's Academy in Taos, Bishop Lammy's school in Santa Fe, N. Mex., College, St. Louis, Mo.; engaged in mercantile pursuits, county judge of Taos County N. Mex., 1875-1880; moved to Ojo Caliente, N. Mex. In 1879; member of the Territorial House of Representatives in 1882; elected as a Democrat to the Forty-ninth and to the four succeeding Congresses (March 4, 1885-March 3, 1895); unsuccessful candidate for reelection in 1894 to the Congress; served in the Territorial Senate 1896-1898; again engaged in the mercantile business; owner of hotels and extensive lands; died in Ojo Caliente April 30, 1910; interment in Fairmount Cemetery, Santa Fe.

Using his birth date and birth location, she tried different ways to find information about his family, but found no Antonio Silva born in Taos. After trying multiple avenues and creative attempts, she still found nothing.

She sat back in her chair and looked at the clock. It was almost midnight and seemed surreal that she had woken up in Mew Mexico that morning. Her head ached and it was hours past her bedtime. Silva was the only concrete name she had, but he was only a bridge to the information she really wanted, which was about the female with "Martina" in her name. Intuitively, Louisa knew she was not Silva's daughter; she was someone who had a very intimate relationship with him. But she could have been anyone—a migrant farm worker's daughter or something. She wondered how on earth she would ever find her.

With a sigh, she turned off the light and walked back through the kitchen, locking the doors and shutting down the house. She grabbed the blanket off the chair and covered Alan, now snoring in his spot on the couch, and went to bed.

She settled into the cold sheets, thankful she had left her socks on. She moved into her normal sleep position, on her left side with a pillow between her knees and one against her chest and stomach, a lingering habit from pregnancy she couldn't seem to break. But her mind raced with thoughts of Silva and the woman in the hammock.

She finally quieted those thoughts, which opened the door for her to fret about a grant that was due at work and how much space all the disposable diapers must take up in land fills. She tossed and turned, and with the final thought about how water moccasins could get into a man-made pond, she began to relax. With each breath, she felt herself falling and caring less and less about water snakes. There was a period of nothingness and then she again found herself in another body.

She sits by a small window. The afternoon sun is shining in, warm on her shoulders. She is in another body again. She holds a black and white photograph of a little girl to her chest. She silently calls out in desperation for someone who isn't there. It was for him; the man she had loved. She is close to the moment of her death.

As Louisa woke up, feelings of desolation overcame her. Tears filled her eyes and she cried into her pillow. Intellectually, she knew she had nothing to be sad about, but the intensity of the emotion in her dream was tangible. Who was this woman, and why was her experience of her so vivid? She got up, wrote down the dream, and then went back to bed.

Journal Entry

February 2003

It has been a month since Malory and I returned from Ojo. I tried several times to find information about Silva and the woman with "Martina" in her name, but life is busy. With two toddlers that seem to have the ability to climb the walls, I often find myself going in circles. It's my busy season at work and my time at home seems to be like *Groundhog Day* the same actions over and over again. Laundry to the washer, then to the dryer. Dishes in the dishwasher, fold the laundry, change a few diapers, unload the dishwasher. After my failed attempts to find the woman, "Martina," I gave up. But my dreams continue and regularly remind me that there are elements to my life that are far from mundane.

At this point I have fully accepted that my relationship to Ojo is a reincarnational one. Reincarnation is an idea I have entertained over the years, which led me to climb up to the attic the other day in search of a journal I kept as a young adolescent. I read with fascination the ideas I played with back then: multiple lives, and that if we are here once, why couldn't we be here two or three times? And there had to be a reason why some people seemed a little more "with it" than others, perhaps because their soul was older and they had already figured some "stuff" out. I then read my theory about the true nature of time. " Time happens over and over again, for every fraction of a second, and all at the same 'time.' This explains deja vu. Our minds get ahead of themselves and when something happens, it feels like it's happened before because it has." This, of course, was how Samantha in Bewitched was capable of traveling back in time, according to my theory.

When I went to college, I started coming across the ideas I held when I was a child. The theory on older souls vs. younger souls related to the karmic wheel in Buddhism. The basic concepts of Quantum physics and the concept of the "holographic universe" related to my ideas about linear time. Perhaps it was Jung's concept of the collective unconscious coming to play. Regardless, it spurred my interest and led to years of informal study. Now, almost twenty years later, I am again entertaining these ideas in a more tangible way than I ever would have thought possible.

For weeks since my return from Ojo, my sleep has been restless and disturbed. In my dreams I have repeatedly found myself in front of the barn. The landscape surrounding it has become very familiar; the large scraggly trees to the left, the smaller trees to the right. Repeatedly I have tried, unsuccessfully, to see what lay to the west of the barn where "she" had slept in the hammock.

There are new images emerging as well, and many nights I wake recalling images of water. Most often I dream of squared off sections of land, and water lay within the low walls that divide the sections as they stair-step down a hill. People are around these squared off sections of land, but I can never recall what they are doing. These fragments replay in my mind like snapshots when I get up to rock Caleb back to sleep or to let the dogs out.

My experiences of the previous year have given me insight to my own dream state. I can't deny the relevance of the name "Silva" coming to me in a dream, and I have learned I can identify by the location and the "tone" of a dream if it's related to Ojo. In fact, all my dreams of that type, regardless of my recognition of the landscape, are identifiable by the way they feel. Over time, these locations have become as easy to discern as any location in my waking life.

Then last night, I had this dream:

I was back in front of the barn; same trees, same blue sky, same landscape. But what's to the left of the barn? I had to get closer. I finally saw it; in front of me was a small adobe house. It had two exterior doors, almost next to each other, similar to a motel. There was a porch, supported by wooden posts across the front of the house, and a few trees blocking my view. I decided to move in closer.

There was a woman giving tours, as if the place was an historic site or museum. She took me past the first door and opened the second door. Looking in, I saw two baby cribs. Both were painted a turquoise blue, but one was very small compared to the other, which was of normal size. "Oh," I said to myself as if remembering, "there were two children, not one. One lived and the other one died as a child." The woman with me affirmed my thoughts. The woman opened the second door and we looked into a bedroom. "And this is where we (meaning the girl and Silva) spent time together." The woman again affirmed my thoughts.

Could the woman in the hammock be another portion of my soul reaching out to me? I have always suspected there was a greater reality in which we all take part and perhaps I am getting a glimpse into it.

11

She is waiting again —for him. She wonders if he will come. She feels anger and disappointment building in the pit of her stomach. She looks around and recognizes what kind of a dream she is having. She is in another body and sitting on a hill, looking down on the crowd. She realizes she has been in this dream before, several times. She looks down at her feet and gathers her skirt tightly around her legs so she can hug her knees. There is activity below and someone emerges in the center of the crowd. She knows it's him and hopes he'll remember his promise to her. As he turns to look up at her, she recognizes him instantly. "You?" she whispers beneath her breath. Knowing her thoughts, he smiles and nods.

Something caused Louisa to stir because she woke up, the dream still resonating in her mind. She looked over at Caleb next to her in the bed and felt his forehead. The poor little guy was cutting molars and had a fever of 103 degrees all day. Then she remembered her dream. Like a new character entering the stage in a play, Matthew had walked into her dream.

Was Matthew a part of a more distant past than the one the two of them had already shared? And it was a long, sorted past that went on for almost a decade before Louisa got married. Oh, the hold he once had on her heart. He was a high school sweetheart, but also a college, graduate school, and early career sweetheart, off and on until their mid twenties. He was the love of her life, or so she thought then. But he was young, immature, and probably more than a little foolish. He had loved her, she did know that, but apparently not enough. The fact that it took her so many years to figure that out indicated she was more than a little foolish too.

The recognition of her dream left her fully awake, so she got up, started her computer and did a search on Ojo Caliente history. She found a website on historic locations in New Mexico and as she scrolled down, she saw that the hotel at Ojo was on the list.

"Let's see here," she said to herself out loud. "It was designed by Antonio Silva and Mrs. Antonio Silva in 1915. She was such a bitch," she stated with firm conviction, feeling her anger building. "Well, she was," Louisa said looking up, explaining her response to the heavens. *Okay Louisa. You are acting like a crazy woman.* But she couldn't deny the way the name "Mrs. Antonio Silva" made her feel.

She went back to bed and tried to quiet her mind. After several minutes, she felt herself relax and her head sank into the pillow. She was almost asleep when she jerked herself awake again. *Did I have a dream?* She couldn't remember. But she knew that the woman with "Martina" in her name was not only deeply intimate with Silva, she was substantially younger than he, and lived with him in a family-like setting. Maybe she was his niece? Louisa got up again and wrote herself a note so she wouldn't forget, grabbed the medicine dropper and Motrin in case Caleb needed it soon, and then slid back under the warm covers.

* * * *

Malory stood in front of the kitchen sink clad in her sock monkey flannel pajamas and socks. It had been a normal Sunday morning with not much activity. She looked out the window above the sink as she washed the dishes from dinner the night before.

She felt a little stir crazy—not because she was bored so much as that it was just a little hard to step back into daily life after her and Louisa's trip to New Mexico, even though it had been more than a month. There was something about them that made her feel so alive yet relaxed. When they were there, it was as if they existed in a suspended state of reality where the mystical was tangible and responsibility was far, far away. It was hard to give that up cold turkey, which would have been helped if she and Louisa had been able to at least go to lunch a few times a week. But she had been sick, Louisa was swamped at work, and then Caleb was sick from cutting teeth. It had been almost three weeks since they had seen each other, which was completely unacceptable.

She rinsed the sponge and wiped out the sink, now done with the kitchen, and picked up the phone to call Louisa.

Louisa was up to her elbows in Comet as she scrubbed the bathtub. When she heard the phone, she pulled off her yellow Playtex glove and ran to the bedroom. "Hello?"

"I'm going insane," said Malory.

"You are?" said Louisa with a laugh, plopping down on the bed. "Do you need to get out for a bit?"

"Maybe. What's your day looking like?"

"I'm just doing housework and hanging with the kids," Louisa said. "Alan is out riding his bike but should be back soon. Do you want to escape and go to a movie or something?"

"Hold on," she said, asking her husband if he minded if she left for a few hours. "It's a go."

A few hours later, the two sat in a booth at Chile's sharing an appetizer and Malory's Diet Coke.

"That movie was so dark," said Louisa. "I just didn't expect it. I had to keep covering my eyes."

"Yeah, we wouldn't want you to be exposed to anything negative," Malory said with a hint of sarcasm as she dipped a southwest egg roll into a side of ranch dressing. "Do you ever watch anything that's not 'G' rated anymore?"

"Probably not."

'You crack me up," said Malory. "Do I have spinach in my teeth?"

"You're good," said Louisa as the waiter showed up with their salads.

"How does everything look ladies?" he asked.

"Can we get a refill on this?" Malory asked holding up her glass.

"Sure. I'll be right back with it."

Louisa sat back in her seat, repositioned her napkin in her lap and stared at her salad. It reminded her of Ojo because they had stopped at the Chile's in Amarillo both going to and coming home from New Mexico in January. That in turn reminded her of her dreams, which made her think about her repeated dreams in which she was waiting for Matthew. She looked up at Malory. "I think Silva is someone I know in this life."

"What?" Malory said, shocked and choking on a piece of lettuce. "Who do you think it is?"

"Matthew," Louisa said as she handed Malory her glass of water to wash down the lettuce. Malory sat back in her seat and took a sip of water. She remembered all the ups and downs he put Louisa through. But they both totally lit up around each other and when they were together, it was like there was no one else in the room. She always thought maybe he just wasn't ready to love Louisa as much as he did. "It is. What made you realize it?" she asked.

"I kept having dreams that I was waiting for someone. They felt like Ojo dreams, but it took a while for me to finally see who I was waiting for. Then the other night I saw who it was."

"It makes so much sense. How did we not consider that possibility?" said Malory, still coughing sporadically and dabbing her eyes. "And why didn't you tell me about these dreams? I can't believe you didn't tell me!"

"I don't know. I think I was in denial." Tears filled Louisa's eyes and she put her hand over her mouth just as the waiter placed the soda in front of Malory.

"Thank you," Malory said to the waiter before he walked away, then turned her attention back to Louisa. "Honey, why are you crying?"

"I'm feeling overwhelmed with emotion. It's just hitting me. It's like I'm a teenager again. I think I have some unresolved issues. I don't think I can even eat this salad. " Louisa used her napkin to dab her eyes.

"Okay. You have unresolved issues."

"Matthew hurt me so much, and so many times—off and on for a decade. And I let him. I kept waiting for him to grow up." Louisa blew her nose into her napkin and wiped her eyes some more.

"So, if Matthew is of the same soul as Antonio…"

"This 'Martina' woman. I have a heightened awareness of her right now. She was very alone. She feels bitter and hard. Her sadness before she died was so intense. She called out to this man in desperation before she died. I know he was never there for her. And he took her child."

"Let's start with Matthew," Malory said. "He was an ass. He was promiscuous and insensitive, but it didn't make your feelings for each other less valid. Here, let me get this off your face." She leaned across the table and pulled a piece of tattered napkin off Louisa's cheek. "Your napkin is shredding."

"Thanks," said Louisa, dusting her cheeks, now paranoid about pieces of her napkin sticking to it. "I always made myself available for him, but he wasn't there for me when I needed him. He got engaged when his mantra was that he wasn't 'ready for a commitment.' That wasn't it at all—I was his security blanket. He used me."

"Well, he never got married," said Malory, "and if I recall some of that had to do with you. Louisa, there was always something very strong between you two."

"I put my life on hold for someone who repeatedly cast me aside. I virtually missed my twenties waiting for him. Do you see the parallels? 'She' waited. I waited."

"If Matthew and Antonio are of the same soul, and this woman is part of 'you,' then it makes sense that there would be parallels," said Malory, reaching over and cutting the chicken on top of Louisa's salad, a gesture intended to encourage eating.

"No. There shouldn't be," Louisa said firmly. "Repeating a pattern? What kind of lousy soul is mine anyway?"

"I'd say it's a pretty amazing soul if you're getting to have this experience."

"This doesn't feel amazing. These old feelings are dredged up and I don't want to feel them." Louisa continued to wipe the tears that streamed down her cheeks. "I tried to put them away and move on with my life and here they are again. I let him treat me like I was disposable. What does that say about my self esteem?"

"Your life, both now and then, is not the life of someone with poor self esteem. You always had your act together. Obviously you two have a connection that was strong enough to follow you into this life." She picked another piece of shredded napkin of Louisa's face.

Louisa thought about a connection that could be strong enough to follow a person into another lifetime as she blew her nose into the rapidly disintegrating napkin. "Maybe that's the point of all these dreams—to help me recognize what's unfinished between us, and what patterns in my life need to be broken?"

"Now you're talking," Malory said, pushing Louisa's salad in front of her now that the chicken was cut into bite-size pieces. "Louisa, she was alone. You're not."

Louisa smiled and reached her hand across the table. Malory took it and squeezed it tight. "What's your hourly rate for therapy?" Louisa asked.

"Give it a few weeks," said Malory. "I'm sure it will be my turn soon."

12

"Hey- Hey!" Alan called in typical fashion as he walked in the door.

"In here!" said Louisa from the kitchen. "Boys, Daddy's home."

"Daddy!" Isaac yelled as he ran toward Alan, Caleb running right behind him.

Louisa looked up from wringing the mop out as Alan made his way into the kitchen. "You have your power clothes on, I see," he said, referring to the business suit she still wore. "Did you have a big meeting today or something?"

"I had to be up at the Capitol."

"*I am woman hear me roar, in numbers too big to ignore,*" Alan sang as he pulled a wine glass out of the cabinet.

"I did no roaring today," she said and mopped around the kitchen table.

"*Oh yes, I am wise, but it's wisdom born of pain. Yes I've paid the price, but look how much I've gained.*" He added a bounce to his step as he moved toward the cabinet where the wine was stored.

"You're the only man I know that sings Helen Reddy songs."

"*If I have to, I can do anything!*"

"It's not normal!" she called over his singing.

"*I am Woman!*" he sang, filling his glass.

"You finished?" asked Louisa, walking back to the sink to rinse out the mop.

"What's not normal is mopping the floor in a skirt and pantyhose," said Alan.

"I got busy, you know, the kids and all. As soon as I'm finished mopping in here can we take them out for a walk? They've been fed and asked if they could throw rocks in the lake."

"Sounds good," he said.

"Okay then. After you drink your wine and we get changed, we'll go. Oh—I know! If it's not too windy we can build a campfire and roast marshmallows."

"Marshmallows!" yelled Isaac.

"Give Daddy a few minutes and then we'll go."

Louisa finished mopping the floor, changed clothes and put jackets on the kids. The four of them walked down to the trail, accompanied by the dogs. The kids ran ahead and Louisa pushed the empty stroller. Aside from the cedar trees, everything was brown and barren in its winter dormancy. Several Canadian geese were on the bank of the small lake, and as the boys grew closer to the trail, the geese honked furiously and swam into the water.

"Alan, I think I am going to try and go back to New Mexico some time next month."

"Why the hell would you do that?"

"I want to continue my research," she said, smiling and stopping to zip up her jacket.

"So you're going to put your needs over those of your family?" He stopped and glared at her with his hands on his hips as she started to walk ahead.

"Don't be silly. How is me going to New Mexico going to be detrimental to the family?" she asked from her place in front of him.

"This marriage is falling apart," Alan replied with disgust, now walking to catch up with her.

"It is?" said Louisa. This was news for her. Quite frankly, she thought they had finally gotten the hang of it.

"I think I wanted a more traditional marriage than I realized," said Alan.

"The only thing untraditional about this marriage is that I earn an income and *still* do everything else," said Louisa. She took a deep breath and felt her blood pressure rising as she realized they were getting ready to more or less have the same argument they'd been having since they were married.

Further up the trail, Louisa saw Caleb fall and heard him cry out from where he fell on the gravel. She ran to him, brushed him off and handed him a stick to redirect his attention. "There you go little man," she said and he ran to catch up with his brother.

Louisa heard Alan approach from behind. "I know what you expect of me, Alan," she said. "I got it."

"Not really," he said. "The only reason you're doing it is because you feel like you have to. It's not what you want, so you'll never truly embrace it."

"You're kidding me, right? It's called compromise. You might try it sometime." Isaac called to her to watch him try and skip a rock. She stopped and watched with a smile as the rock plopped into the water. "Good try sweetie." They started walking again.

"See, that's what I mean. You're doing it, but it's not in your heart. I'm the man. I should be able to come and go as I please and trust that you'll take care of things."

"You already come and go as you please and trust that I'll take care of things."

"When I bark or snap, you should jump. That means I'm here," he gestured with his hand, "and you're here," he said, indicating her place beneath him.

"Give me a break," said Louisa. "Nothing before we got married in any way indicated that you believed I was inherently beneath you."

"We weren't married then. But you should take this as a compliment. I trust you to handle these things. If I didn't, I would do them myself."

"So you're delegating?" she asked condescendingly, which seemed to bypass him altogether.

"Yes. That's a good way to put it," he said.

"Okay honey. I'm curious. When we were at the altar and said 'I do,' did your status immediately rise, or did mine immediately fall?" Louisa asked, but didn't get an answer. She turned the stroller back toward the house and called for the kids. "Listen. I feel like we've finally found a balance that works. I've been cooperative. Your statement about being inherently 'above' me is ridiculous and that's where I stand on this matter. Got it? I can't do any more than I already am."

Before he could respond, the boys came running toward them with sticks in their hands. "What are you guys doing?" Alan asked, bending down to their level as they put the wood in the stroller.

"Campfire," said Caleb.

"Good thinking," said Alan. He looked up at Louisa and smiled. "At least we have great kids."

Louisa gave the boys a smile and tussled Isaac's hair. She watched as the kids ran ahead with their dad and felt the tears building in her eyes. She thought over the past several weeks. She recalled her conversation with Malory about Matthew and the way she was, years after the fact, working through that relationship. She was mad, at herself as much as anyone. She let herself be treated like she was of little value with Matthew, and now Alan tells her she's in some way beneath him? Alan, Matthew, Silva. If this was a pattern for her, it was time for that pattern to change.

* * * *

Louisa gave herself a few days to let the dust from her argument with Alan settle. She knew better than to make any grand determinations of her feelings about him when she was angry. He could be a real ass, but then he'd turn around and cheer her on about a goal at work, tell her she was the best person he could have chosen to be the mother of his children, or serenade her "I am Woman" by Helen Reddy. Those things fell into the category of reasons she married him, so she knew not to be hasty.

But regardless of his intention, his words and attitude triggered recognition for her. Recognition of not only patterns but also of how much of her "self" she was willing to give up to be in a relationship, and more recently had been setting aside in the process of being a wife and mother. A few days away were not unreasonable or neglectful of the kids and she determined she would be going back to Ojo for a "research trip."

She would start with the core of the subject matter at hand: multiple lives. She sat on the floor of the bookstore in front of the book shelves labeled "New Age." She felt overwhelmed by the size of it. She could remember a time when this section was an end-shelf labeled "Occult" with just a few titles on it. But that was twenty years ago and now there were too many gurus to count. How, with hundreds of books to choose from, would she find the right one to give her the insight she needed to help her better understand what she had been experiencing?

She closed her eyes. "Spirit," she silently called. "I know you have been speaking to me. Please guide me to where there is information I can benefit from right now. Amen."

She continued to sit for a few moments with her eyes closed. She felt a tug toward the far bottom corner on the right. She opened her eyes and crawled over to the far right corner of the shelf. Scanning the few books in the corner, she saw it and smiled.

Seth Speaks by Jane Roberts. Why hadn't she thought of that? She pulled the book off the shelf and examined the watercolor design on the cover, quite different from the copy she bought at a garage sale her first year of college. Jane Roberts, she had learned the first time she tried to read the book, was a gifted channeler during the sixties and seventies. Seth was the "personality" that spoke through Jane and the book was one of several documenting the sessions. Louisa remembered it had taken her several attempts to get through the book because the material was unlike anything she had ever read before.

She sat back down in the aisle and flipped through the pages, looking for the chapter headings. "Chapter One: I Don't Have A Body Yet I Am Writing This Book." She chuckled. *This is some far out stuff.* She continued to flip through, past chapter two, chapter three, and stopped at chapter four. "Reincarnational Dramas." She skimmed the first few pages, gave a silent "thank you" for the guidance, and took the book to the counter.

Later that night when the house was quiet, Louisa went into the bedroom and began reading.

> "Consider yourself as an actor in a play; hardly a new analogy, but a suitable one. The scene is set in the twentieth century. You create the props, the setting, the theme; in fact you write, produce, and act the entire production—you and every individual who takes part. You are so focused in your roles, however, so intrigued by the reality you have created, so entranced by the problems, challenges, hopes and sorrows of your particular role that you have forgotten they are of your own creation.

> But there are other plays going on simultaneously, in which you also have a part to play. These have their own scenery and props. They take place in different periods of time… [You] are so focused within this drama that you are not aware of the others in which you play a role. You do not understand your own multidimensional reality, therefore it seems strange when I tell you that you live many existences at one time.

> Now these various plays, these creative period pieces represent what you would call reincarnational lives. They all exist basically at one time. They seem to be taking place one after the other, intensifying the false idea that time is a series of moments, passing in a single line."[1]

Louisa pulled out the notebook that contained her research and dream documentation. Finding a clean page of paper, she jotted down some notes and continued to read about the assumptions we have about existence, such as that we exist in an objective world that is independent of our own creativity and perception, that time is a series of moments, and that we are limited by space and time. When she got

---

[1] Roberts, Jane. *Seth Speaks: The Eternal Validity of the Soul*. California: Amber Allen Publishing and New World Library, 1972, pp. 46-48.

to a section about problems and progress, her spine tickled with a nervous energy and she knew she needed to pay close attention.

> "…These plays are highly spontaneous affairs in which the actor has full freedom. In each play, individually and *en masse*, different problems are set up.
>
> Progress can be measured in terms of the particular ways those problems are solved or not solved. Progress has nothing to do with time, you see, but psychic and spiritual forces…It is not correct to suppose that your actions in this life are caused by your actions in a previous existence, or that you are being punished in this life for a crime in a past one. The lives are simultaneous. There is instant communication and an instant, if you prefer, feedback system.
>
> These plays are hardly without purpose. In them the multidimensional personality learns through its own actions. It tries out an endless variety of poses, behavior patterns, attitudes, and changes others as a result."[2]

She lay back on her pillows and contemplated what she read about an instant feedback system between other "selves." She tried to wrap her mind around the possibilities that lie in karma being simultaneous; that effects of an action in one lifetime might cut across space and time affecting another in that "moment." Was there a constant interplay? How might this apply to her experiences? She picked up the book and read on.

> "…He (the actor) is not left, abandoned within a play which he has forgotten is his own creation. He has knowledge and information that comes to him through what I call the inner senses…[There are periods in which] he understands that he had his hand in writing the play, and is freed from those assumptions that bind him while he is actively concerned with the drama's activities. These periods, of course, coincide with your sleep states and dreaming conditions.

---

[2] (Roberts, pp. 48-50)

The purpose of any given life is available to you, the knowledge beneath the surface of the conscious self you know...You have knowledge of your <u>entire</u> multidimensional personality at your fingertips...<u>When</u> you realize that you do, this knowledge allows you to solve problems or meet the challenges you have set, quicker, in your terms..."[3]

She silently repeated what she read. *When you realize that you do have this knowledge, it allows you to solve the problems or meet the challenges you have set more quickly.* Perhaps that was a part of what was happening; she was recognizing that she had the knowledge, enabling her to better meet the challenges she had set for herself.

She marked her page, set her work on the night table and turned out the light.

---

[3] (Roberts, pp. 50-51)

13

It was a cold, dreary day and rain pattered on the windshield as she pulled into the parking lot in front of Alan's office. She wasn't there to see him, but it was an available space close to the Thai restaurant next to his office where she was meeting Malory for lunch. She grabbed her umbrella and quickly opened it as she stepped into the rain and ran for the restaurant.

Malory was already seated and waved to Louisa when she walked in the door. On the table sat a plate of fried tofu and a cup of hot tea in front of Louisa's spot.

"How did you know I'd want ginger peach tea today? You're a mind reader," said Louisa, bending down to give Malory a hug.

"I figured you'd be cold," she said. "I feel like I haven't seen you in forever. What's been going on?"

"Lots that I don't want to go into," said Louisa, referring to the Cold War going on between her and Alan. She dipped a piece of tofu in some peanut sauce. "But I'm going back to New Mexico. Or maybe I should restate that. We are going back to New Mexico, if you will join me. I want to do some research, and as my Ojo partner, I want you with me."

"Absolutely! When are we going?"

"In April. I set some money aside last month and will this month as well, and then I'll just have to check work and make sure the boys are covered. I just told Alan the other night. We need to look at our calendars." Louisa reached for Malory's soda.

"When are you going to break down and realize you like Diet Coke with Thai food?" Malory asked, handing Louisa her glass.

"I might acknowledge that soon," she said, taking a sip. "But why is it necessary when you enable me by letting me drink yours?"

Malory smiled. "Let's talk about this research. Where do you want to start?"

"This idea just came to me, so I haven't formulated that yet," Louisa said. "The one thing I do know is that I want to make the hike up to Posi. I started to on our last trip but felt uneasy."

"I remember. What exactly is Posi anyway?" Malory asked. "I gather it's some type of archaeological site, but that's all I know."

"I have no idea either. Maybe we should do a search and see what comes up. Let's pop in and use Alan's computer before I head back to the office."

When they finished lunch, they went next door and sat in Alan's office. Alan was gone, so Louisa sat down in the chair at his desk.

"Let me type," said Malory, nudging Louisa out of the chair. "I'm faster and you have to get back to work."

"Alright," Louisa said, giving Malory the chair. "I'm not that slow, you know."

"You're an amazing woman with other strengths."

"Thank you."

"I'm just amazed you never took typing," said Malory.

"Just do the search."

Malory typed "Posi, New Mexico." Only a few things came up and each made reference to "Posi-Ouinge" and "Hupobi-Ouinge."

"Well, this has to be it," said Louisa, pointing at one of the listings. Malory clicked on the link.

The website popped up on the monitor and Malory read out loud. "Both 'Posi' and 'Hupobi' are archeological sites of the early Tewa Indians who inhabited the Ojo Caliente basin prior to the Spanish invasion," read Malory. "The sights are within a mile of one another, on opposite sides of the mineral springs." She then clicked the mouse on a listing titled "the Hupobi Heritage Project."

"Oh my gosh," whispered Louisa as she looked at the monitor from over Malory's shoulder. It was an artist's reconstruction of the early pueblo, including drawings of terraced gardens used to grow their crops. She instantly recognized the squared levels from her dreams.

"Louisa, this picture looks like what you drew for me when you told me about the levels of water you were dreaming about," said Malory, looking back at Louisa with surprise. "Those are terraced gardens."

"I don't know what to make of it. Terraced gardens? How on earth would I come up with that?" asked Louisa, kneeling on the ground next to the chair so she could see better.

"Maybe you didn't 'come up with it,'" Malory said, "maybe you're remembering it."

"What is the exact location of Hupobi?"

"This says it is just northwest of the school there. Wait a minute," Malory said, turning to Louisa and smiling.

Louisa's eyes widened with recognition. "That's where we pulled off the road and hiked down to the river in January. Do you remember the sign for the school? Hupobi's right there?"

"I think it's safe to say what was pulling you that day," said Malory. "You followed your gut, and without knowing it, it led you there. I love it!"

"But wait," said Louisa, "Silva lived in the 1800s. This says Hupobi was inhabited before the 1300s. I don't understand. That would mean—"

"Oh my god. There's more than one," said Malory.

Louisa recalled learning about the tribes which lived along the Chama River. She had set the information aside because of the dream about the baby "Silva" since the name was the only concrete piece of information she had.

Were there three people, including Louisa, in the same location but in different time periods? It was as if a convergence was happening in this "random" location Alan had sent her the year before.

14

Alan walked into the lit bedroom and saw Louisa curled up on her side, asleep. It was well after midnight and he had been working at the computer all night. As he walked around the bed to turn off the light, he saw she was holding a pencil and had a notebook next to her. He flipped through the pages and saw it contained notes from her dreams. She had told him the stories, but quite frankly, he didn't listen closely enough to keep up with what had been going on. Something about a guy in a picture, some ghosts. And he wasn't happy about the fact that she was going to be leaving him with the kids again, which led him to be even less inclined to show an interest.

Before he put the notebook down, he noticed she had written down a dream that night, which must have been why the light was on. He began to read.

Dream: March 15, 2003

I feel the springs in the distance and know I am close to Ojo. There are people everywhere, doing tasks and milling about. There's a group under a covered structure and they are talking and laughing. I see my friend Lea and within my dream ask myself, "What's she doing here?" I watch her from a distance. We are then in a different location and she is searching for a box that belonged to her mother.

I opened my eyes and looked at the clock. It was 11:30. I rolled over to go back to sleep and quickly slipped back into my dream:

We are in a cave. A male authority figure sits in front of me. It's Kara, the Director of a program like mine in another part of the state, just like Lea. I know it is an Ojo dream by how it feels, but what is Kara doing there? And she's a man? Kara gave me my instructions: find where someone is and report back. The instructions were firm. I leave and then find myself somewhere watching people. They see me so I run. I am again in another body, and she is running and breathing hard. I can feel the rush of fear and panic as the girl whose body I'm in tries to get away. She is close to safety but can't outrun them.

When I startled out of sleep, I felt a sting in the fold of my arm. I turned on the light to look and saw tracks of blood. I can only conclude that I was digging into my arms because there is blood under my fingernails.

Alan placed the notebook onto the nightstand and saw a pair of scissors next to what looked like the foot sections of a pair of socks. For a moment he was confused, until he noticed that Louisa had cut the feet out of the socks to make bands for her arms. He gently pulled one down so as not to wake her and saw the scratch marks she had written about. He laughed to himself, then shook his head in dismay and remembered what he thought right after they got married. He had no idea how their marriage would pan out, but he knew one thing for certain—he would never get bored.

* * * *

Louisa sat on the floor in the bathroom with her back against the tub and looked up at the sink, unsure of how she got there. She held a washcloth on her arm and, taking it off, saw that she had scratched herself again. It had been two weeks of bizarre dreams and if she forgot to put her sock bands on, she inevitably dug into her arms. She put the cool cloth on the back of her neck and retraced the events that may have led her to the bathroom floor.

Had she been dreaming about Kara again? Or was she feeling the residue from their conversation earlier in the day? Louisa had called her to find out if she had ever spent any time in New Mexico, which she had. Not only that, Kara shared her experience at Bandalier National Monument, northwest of Santa Fe. She told Louisa that when she was there, she got physically ill—nauseous and so dizzy she had to sit down. What was stranger, though, was that she also had a vision. She said she "saw" people around, some working and children playing. Then everything went black. When the scene came back everyone was gone. She said she was filled with sadness and felt like she was seeing it all from the perspective of an older man.

As Louisa got her bearings, she had to think to remember how she ended up in the bathroom. Her arm was stinging when she began to wake up. Still half asleep, she walked to the bathroom, but at the same time, it was as if she was dreaming. *She's running.* She turned on the faucet and grabbed a washcloth. *She sees the familiar mountainous landscape and hears the men behind her.* She wrapped the washcloth around the fold in her arm, her head spinning. *Two men tackled her to the ground. "They're going to kill me."* Louisa slid down to the floor with her back against the bathtub. *She is sitting on the ground with her back against a tree. There are ropes cutting into her arms.* It was the ropes around her arms—she was scratching at the ropes in her sleep. In the instant of that realization, there was a swirling of images closing in on her like a hologram. They, these people she worked with, were the tribe.

Exhausted, she pulled a towel off the rack, covered herself, and curled up in a ball on the floor.

The next morning, Louisa stopped by Malory's house before work. She sat in her favorite rocker next to the gas fireplace in Malory's living room and told her about the dreams, Kara and Lea, and the scratch marks on her arms. "After I was in the other body and her arms were tied behind her back, more pieces came together in a fraction of a second; the dream about Kara giving me instructions and then getting captured; the dream about Lea in Ojo Caliente and a conversation about her mother who had recently died while there, and Kara's experience at Bandelier…"

"Oh my God," Malory blurted. "The tribe—the tribe came back. I've read about this, where groups of people come together in loose formations over and over again. Do you think the dream was the 'Martina' woman?"

"No. The dream I had about Kara giving me instructions—the spying, the being chased? I think this is the one who was drowned. I think I'm having a brain dump right now," Louisa said, looking down at her watch. "Damn. I'm going to have to go soon."

"So how do you know the difference when you have dream experiences about these people?" asked Malory.

"The tone is different, and the ones about the Indian woman 'feel' farther away—maybe my way of making sense of how long ago she lived."

Malory nodded contemplatively. "Well, it's been an amazing few months and we leave in three weeks. Are you ready for the ride?"

*   *   *   *

She feels someone bending over her and whispering in her ear. "Ma-Wi-Taa." Louisa's eyes fly open. She sits up and looks over her shoulder. It was so physical. So real. She knows it's a name; that of the woman who was drowned. Maybe it was "Martina"? No. This is different. She lies back down, closes her eyes, and drifts back into sleep.

Ma-Wi-Taa

15

She stood in front of the respected elder inside the narrow cave. The morning sun shone brightly outside, but in the shadowy light of the cave, she could barely make out the ancient sketches on the wall and the blackened ceiling that indicated it had once been the home of a lone cliff dweller. She had made the journey alone, knowing that her life was in danger by making it.

"You must travel south along the river then west to the abandoned village," he said to her in broken Tewa. "A band of Spanish soldiers camp there. Learn how many and what weapons they have."

"And then?" Ma-Wi-Taa asked.

"Return when the sun is high in one day. If you are followed, lead them away from the cave."

She bowed her head to the respected elder and made her way out into the slowly increasing daylight.

The elder warrior was from a tribe that was enemy to hers. Not long before the Spanish returned and her people were forced to take refuge on top of the dark mesa, their tribes had been at war. But desperation changes alliances and she understood the greater enemies were the soldiers that returned to take their home.

The hot summer sun beat down on the top of her head as she made her way southward and her black hair absorbed the heat. She knelt by the water to fill her water pouch. The deer gut swelled as the water ran into it and she poured some over her head.

She turned around and looked in the direction of the mesa where her clan was and wondered if her father would be angry she was helping an "enemy" in trying to defeat the Spanish. When they had returned and her people took to high ground, she had disagreed. Should they not fight to their deaths rather than live a life of slavery and lose the lands that were their home as they had before? Now she went against the wishes of her clan.

The sun moved farther down in the sky as she approached the abandoned village. It was still a distance, but she heard voices. Crouching in the trees, she saw two men. They were hunting and one had just shot a rabbit. They talked and laughed between themselves as they made their way southward to where their horses were. She followed behind them, trying to recall what Spanish she had learned as a child to understand what they were saying.

She made her way toward the back side of the village and found a place on the hillside where she thought she would be out of view. Looking down, she saw there was a group of six men, all with horses. She saw harquebuses scattered around the camp where they had set them down, obviously not worried about an attack. She then looked farther to the left where she saw two mules and a small wagon. There was a wooden box and some large bundles. More weapons, perhaps? If so, a few would be helpful for the Indians in comparison to their sling shots and arrows. She decided to move closer to get a better look.

Dropping to her stomach, she crept through the tall grass, and as she pulled herself up behind a small piñon tree, she heard a yell. The six men turned in unison and one pointed in her direction. Two headed up the hillside on foot and the others mounted their horses, yelling as they made their way toward her.

She jumped up and started running. Fear and panic coursed through her veins as she ran down the mountainside, looking for someplace that would protect her. Her footpace was no match for them and she could hear the sound of horse hooves. She heard a voice behind her, and one jumped off his horse and ran after her, pulling her to the ground.

The second man on horseback swung himself to the ground and brought over some rope, tying her hands together and placing more in a noose around her neck. Her mind was racing. Were they going to kill her?

The third man on horseback slowly approached the others. He dismounted and walked in their direction, just as the two on foot scrambled breathlessly over the ridge into view. Looking at her, he took the ropes in his hands. "You two take my horse back to camp," he said, gesturing to the men on foot. "I'll walk her down."

* * * * *

The groundwork for that fateful moment was laid more than a century and a half earlier, when the Spanish first crossed into the land of the Pueblo people from Mexico in search of the rumored cities of gold. It would take nearly fifty years for the Spanish to successfully conquer her people, but once they did, parts of their way of life would be lost forever. In the end, they would essentially live in slavery. Their children were taken from them, women were raped, they were forced to build the very churches that would replace their centers of worship, and would be punished and tortured for practicing their own religion.

She had seen eleven winters and ten summers when the runners had come with the knotted yucca cords. They came with a message from Popé, the great Tewa Shaman, who had been one of forty- nine men taken captive by the Spanish as examples for practicing their religion. Escaping hanging, he was released when a group of northern tribal warriors made threats upon Santa Fe, and over the next five years he devised a plan for revenge. The message sent was that each Pueblo was to, in secret, untie one knot each day until there were no more, which meant it was time for battle.

Across the Pueblo world, enemy tribes united to take back their land from the Spanish. The surprise attack spared no one. More than four hundred Spanish settlers were killed, but the most brutal torture was saved for the twenty one priests. After the attacks, Ma-Wi-Taa's father, brothers and uncles, traveled south to where the Spanish were barricaded within the walls of Santa Fe. She heard of men that never returned, but remembered the day her father walked back into their village, saying that the Spanish had gone south and that life would be better now.

After eighty years of oppression and leadership from the outside, something new had to be created to take its place. And while some of the elders spoke of what their parents had told them of the old ways, no one alive really knew the entirety of how their ancestors lived.

A council was formed to unite the pueblos and Popé was named chief. Tribal strife led to him being deposed, as was his successor. The next chief led an attack on the Hopi to the west. Then the Hopi and Zuni were at war. The Tiwa from Taos, the Keres pueblos, and Pecos took up war against her people, the Tewa. Life was no more peaceful than before the revolt. There were droughts and famine, and the Apaches and Navajos from the north continued their raids with increasing severity to access whatever grain was kept in storage within the pueblos. The villages that had so strongly united in her childhood had grown weak in their solidarity. She experienced the chaos and struggles that accompanied their liberation. While that freedom had held a cost, it was something she believed in and would come to learn she would fight for.

She lived in a village just south of where the small river merges with the bigger waters. Her family had lived in the area as far back as anyone could recall and she herself felt an inexplicable connection to the land and to the ancestors that had preceded her. She often made the journey to where they had lived until one hundred years earlier at Puye, the ruins where the rabbits gather. When the springs dried up, the clans had moved on, but she could still feel the ancestors there; in the cliff dwellings dug into the walls of the sandstone mountain, the ceilings still blackened from their fires, and in the stacked stone walls of the Great House still intact on top of the mesa. From there she could see for miles; the rolling cliffs and small mountains spotted with green shrub, the deep blue of the sky, the sacred mountains in each direction. There she could listen for guidance on how life could be better for her people.

Her Catholic name given upon baptism was Isabella, meaning "God is my oath," but her oath would never be to the God the priests spoke of. Her people called her Ma-Wi-Taa. Though as a female she could never go through the training of the Shamans, she was gifted in those ways, as well as with plants and their uses to heal. She studied and served under the medicine man of her village. This responsibility often took her away from home and the daily life inherent in it, giving her spirit a sense of freedom as if it rode the current of the river or drifted in the wind. She went where she was needed when she was needed, otherwise spending time in solitude communing with the Ancestors.

She was joined in union at fifteen to a young warrior named Running Bear. Both away from the village often; she to do her work and he to do his, standing guard from high posts watching for possible attack from the villages that had waged war upon them, or spotting Navajo and Apache raiders. Their life together was brief; only three years. He was killed by a band of Apache that took him off guard one night when the moon was new. Less than a year later, their infant child fell ill, and his Soul traveled the sacred road to the Spirits.

Ma-Wi-Taa's grief immense, she retreated inside herself. There she would stay for the next several sun cycles. But the scent of change was on the breeze, and while she could feel it, she had no way of fathoming the extent of change to come; now twelve years after her people took back their home.

16

She sat grinding sage when she looked up to see a runner coming; like a moving dot coming down the hill. A sense of foreboding filled her chest and she stood and walked toward the southernmost entrance to the pueblo. As he came closer, she saw it wasn't one of her tribe; something must have happened. Visions of horror still filled her imagination from the Spanish massacre at Zia not a year earlier, where eighty soldiers killed more than six hundred Zia men, women and children. Then they learned that Santa Fe had been taken back by the Spanish and the troops made their way to each pueblo, erected crosses, and the priests again baptized more than two thousand pueblo people.

But the Spanish hadn't stayed, and the rumor quickly spread throughout the Pueblo world that when they returned, they would kill every man old enough to have taken part in the revolt more than a decade earlier. The Tewa had tried to prepare by forming loose alliances with tribes that were otherwise their enemies.

As the runner came into the village, dogs nipped at his heels as he ran toward an elder, requesting to speak with the Chief. Questions of what had happened came from the growing crowd around him, and they learned that the troops had returned, but this time they brought settlers and were camped outside the walls of Santa Fe.

As the warriors said goodbye to their families, Ma-Wi-Taa watched with sadness, wondering if they, too, would meet a fate similar to that of the people at Zia.

* * * *

A cold, dreary month passed before the warriors returned. When word spread about the battle in Santa Fe, the executions, and the forced slavery of all else that remained, Ma-Wi-Taa's people had fled, by the hundreds, from the surrounding Pueblos near the river. They took refuge on the top of the remote, dark mesa not far from her home. With steep cliffs surrounding most of it as it rose hundreds of feet in the air, there was only one steep trail that could be navigated to reach the top.

It was a brutally cold winter, but they took shelter in the makeshift homes they built with dirt and rocks. The sun rose and fell almost sixty times before the Spanish army was discovered at the base of their refuge. They attempted battle, but the heavy snow made shooting their weapons difficult and ascending the butte impossible. When attempts were made, the Tewa warriors used slingshots and threw rocks, proving much more effective from their heights than in a land battle. The enemy remained there for three weeks before they gave up and moved back toward Santa Fe.

Throughout the pueblo world, the refugees took to high lands for protection. Winter moved into spring and there they remained. But some had to make their way down; to hunt and to get water when the rain and snow stopped. Messengers were sent to communicate with others, and Ma-Wi-Taa gathered the plants and roots needed to help her people, many suffering from illness and famine. With each descent from the mesa, she felt more and more comfortable and confident, and over time she wandered farther away from the base of the mesa.

It was one such day that she left at dawn. As she traveled along the river, she saw a young man exiting a large crevice in a rock formation in the distance. She waded across the river in his direction to get a closer look, and as she made her way through the cottonwood trees, he almost ran into her.

Startled, he said, "It is not safe out here. You should go back where you came from," in broken Tewa.

"I have seen nothing dangerous. I heard they are fighting toward the sunsets," she responded.

"Yes, but there are others now. Small groups of them. They have been taking belongings and the grain that is still stored at the pueblos. They have killed many of our people and the troops are coming back this way. We were on Kotyiti, to the south. They came, the warriors fled to higher ground and then attacked. Many of the captives were then able to run."

He was Keres, a tribe now enemy to the Tewa. She took in what he was saying and cautiously took a step back. "What are you doing in Tewa lands? Are you not scared for your life?" Then gesturing toward the rocks, "What were you doing in the cave?"

"There is an elder warrior hiding there," he continued. "He is angry and knows the Spanish will be coming this way to finish the Tewa. You should go back to safety." The young man backed away and broke into a swift run down the river.

Ma-Wi-Taa turned and looked up at the opening in the rocks. Turning back again, she waded across the river and made her way back to the mesa. She knew then that she would return, climb to the crevice between the large rocks, and become a part of this attempt to take back their homeland.

Louisa

17

Louisa looked at the clock. It was just before noon and the rest of her staff had left for lunch. The office was suddenly quiet. She had some time before her scheduled meeting and since she was leaving for New Mexico in two weeks, she decided she had better start her pre-trip research. But first she checked her e-mail.

"Of course I hear from you now," she said out loud when she saw a message from Matthew. "Have you felt me working through our past?"

He wrote to tell her that a friend's mother had died from flu complications. She was young and her death was sudden and unexpected. When he heard about it, it made him realize how sad he would be if something happened to Louisa and they never got to say goodbye.

She responded: "Hi. Good to hear from you. I have thought about the same thing before, that one of us will hear after the fact that the other has passed. But you can always know that I love you very much, regardless of if we are in contact or not. Let me know how you are and what you have been up to."

She again looked at the clock and saw she had fifteen minutes until she needed to leave for her meeting. Having learned about Hupobi and the terraced gardens, she knew she wanted to try and visit the site. She decided finding out if it was open to the public was a starting point for her pre-trip research.

First she came across a website for Anthropology day trips through a museum in Santa Fe and learned there was going to be a class in October that visited both Posi and Hupobi. *That could be cool.* She made a mental note of it and went on to see if she could get details about Hupobi, but found nothing. She then tried the Taos Historical Society, as the pueblo was located in present day Taos County, but found nothing but information on Rancho de Taos. She scrolled down and saw a link to a website that was focused on New Mexico genealogy and history. With a "click" the homepage was on the screen, and before her was a list of honorary members of the Historical Society. Antonio Silva was the first name on the list. She smiled to herself that she might finally be on to something helpful.

Louisa quickly inspected the site. There was data from the 1910 census, fragments of letters and historical documents, and maps of the county lines before they were changed to present day counties. She made the mental note that Taos and Rio Arriba county lines were right at the Ojo Caliente mark on the map.

She then saw you could submit a name and a volunteer would do a Census search. *Maybe I can find some information on Silva and his family.* She typed his name, date of birth and death, and that he was born in Taos County and sent off her request. She glanced at the clock, wrote down the web address and left for her meeting.

The following morning, Louisa went by Malory's after taking the kids to breakfast before nursery school. It was cold and windy, so Malory put on the kettle to make some tea. "So what's been going on?"

"Let's see," said Louisa searching her memory as she moved a stack of newspapers from the chair to the kitchen table and sat down. "Not a whole lot. Things at work have been unusually smooth, which is nice. What about you? How are things with Scott?"

"Nothing's really changed, but I think I'm having a renaissance infatuation."

"I'd say every couple needs that once in a while," said Louisa, smiling.

"Tell me about it. This may be a one sided renaissance infatuation, but I'll take it."

"As you should," said Louisa. "Hey, I forgot to tell you I started some pre-trip research yesterday and came across this really great website that has information on Taos County from the 1800's."

"I want to see this right now," said Malory, immediately walking toward the back of the house. Louisa picked up her mug and followed Malory into the office, which was a catch-all room for any items that needed to be either given or thrown away.

"Honey, I keep telling you, we could knock this room out in one day if you'd let me help you," Louisa said as she made her way through the clutter and back to the desk. "We'd make three piles: keep, giveaway, and trash. It would be so gratifying. Can you feel the purge?"

"I know. The task just overwhelms me."

"That's why you need to ask me for help," Louisa said, pulling over a chair. "Okay, are you ready for the address?"

Malory quickly typed as Louisa read it to her. "This could be some great stuff," she said excitedly. "How did you find this?"

"One thing led to another and this is where I ended up. Remember all the trouble I had initially? Call me crazy, but it felt as if things opened up— like the Universe said, 'okay, you're ready.'"

"You've had a lot of dreams and realizations since our January trip. Maybe you needed that as a foundation."

"Maybe so."

"There's a lot of great information here," said Malory. "Did you get a chance to look at this list of Spanish surnames?"

"No. I had to leave for my meeting so I didn't get to look at this in depth."

"Well, now seems like a good time if you're ready."

"I feel nervous," said Louisa.

"Maybe that means you're close to something," said Malory, clapping her hands together excitedly. "Okay, surnames. Silva isn't here. That's interesting. He must not have been Spanish."

"That makes it easier, doesn't it?" said Louisa. "If it's not a surname, there likely won't be very many of them."

"Good thinking. Let's look at the information on the postmasters for Ojo Caliente."

"Look here," Louisa said quickly, leaning over Malory to point at the monitor. "It says the post office was opened in 1870, it closed after two years, and was reopened in 1881 by a man named Anthony Silva. He and a John Silva held the position for several years, and then an Anthony F. Silva held it several years later. Ojo Caliente couldn't have been that big of a town. These men have to be family members to Antonio."

"Hmmm. Interesting," Malory responded as she moved around the site.

"Click on this," Louisa said, pointing to the link for the 1910 census. "This is so cool. I need to take some time and look through this page by page."

"Let's just do it now. I bet it won't take too long to scan each page."

"Are you sure?" Louisa asked. "There are more than a hundred pages. It could take a while."

"Not with both of us doing it," said Malory. "Any time we come across the Silva name, let's write down all the information." She handed Louisa a piece of paper and a pencil.

"Okay. You click, I'll write," Louisa said, and they proceeded through each page. Each time the "Silva" name came up, Louisa wrote down the information. All in all, there were only three Silva families in the area at that time.

"But where is Antonio?" asked Malory. "If he started the business at the springs, he should be here."

"Remember the information I found on him right after we got back in January? I think he died in 1910. He may have passed before the census was taken." Louisa paused and reviewed her notes. "Looking at the ages of some of these people, this John Silva must have been a brother or cousin of Antonio's. Here is a woman named Libby Silva who lived with her son and his very young wife. His name was Anthony, so likely the one that served as postmaster after 1900. Next to Libby's name, the census said she owned a mercantile. Didn't Antonio own the mercantile?"

"Louisa, if he already died, that was probably his wife, and Anthony was his son."

"I don't like her," Louisa said, referring to Mrs. Antonio Silva.

"You are cracking me up! You rarely talk like that about people," Malory replied.

"She wasn't nice. Ah! I'm frustrated. How am I ever going to find the 'Martina' woman?"

"Tell me what you think about her again?"

"I think part of her name sounds like 'Martina.' There is definitely a 't' in it. She had a very intimate relationship with Silva. I think she was much younger than he, and lived with him, like she was a niece or something. I know it sounds crazy, but that's my gut feeling. I think she had a baby with him and that he gave the baby to his brother. The baby would have been illegitimate because he was married."

"Well, let's just keep looking. We're just getting started, and if you believe that these avenues are opening up because it's time, you have to have trust."

"Malory, how am I so fortunate to have a friend like you to share this experience with me?"

"I wouldn't miss it for the world."

"All of the sudden I'm starving," said Louisa.

"Me too. I've got chocolate chip cookie dough in the fridge."

"Sounds great. Can I check my e-mail? Even though I'm not at work, I want to stay on top of things."

"Sure. I'm going to grab a Diet Coke, too."

Louisa saw there was nothing that needed her attention at the office and when Malory sat back down, she was checking her personal mail. "What do you know? An e-mail from Matthew."

"Antonio must have sensed us trying to find him," Malory said with a coy smile. "What does he have to say?"

"Nothing important. He was checking in to see how I was doing."

"Have you told him about all this?" asked Malory, pouring her soda into a tall glass of ice.

"No." Louisa scooped a spoonful of cookie dough and leaned back in the chair.

"Are you going to?" asked Malory.

"I don't know. Apparently these late adolescent emotions still run pretty deep," Louisa said dryly with self deprecating humor as she took another bite of cookie dough.

"I see," said Malory.

"But," said Louisa, "if I step back and observe things from a distance: the dreams, the research, the realizations and parallels I feel about he and I and the woman and Antonio—well, it's pretty interesting to see it unfold. He's been keeping in closer contact than he has in years, though, which I find interesting."

"Synchronicity."

"Speaking of synchronicity," said Louisa as she sat up and looked at the rest of her e-mail listings. "Look what else is here— perfect timing. Can I print this?"

"Sure. What are you talking about?"

"I e-mailed a volunteer through the web site we have been looking at. I sent her Antonio's name and birth information for a census search."

"You didn't tell me you did that!" Malory said with pseudo indignation.

"Sorry babe. But since the information's here, let's look at it."

Hi Louisa,

> *I ran across your Anthony in the 1850 census in Taos in the household of his parents as follows:*

> *1850 Census N. Division, Taos, NM. Territory, page 157A, Enumerated on Dec. 2nd , Dwelling and family #1307.*

> *Peter Silva. Age 37, Merchant, born in Island St. (unreadable) Azores Islands, Portugal.*

> *Anna, wife, age 21, born in AL*

> *Antonio, age 6, born in MO*

John, age 3 born in Taos, New Mexico Territory

I am not positive about his mother's name, but it appears to be Anna. There are four other non-relative people living on the property as laborers and one carpenter. He must have been having his house built.

"Antonio was referred to as Anthony," said Louisa. "How did we miss that? And he wasn't born in Taos County, which would explain why I kept hitting a dead end. The Political Graveyard has misinformation."

"Get the notes. Let's redo this family tree," Malory said. "Okay. John was Antonio's brother, as we suspected."

"And their father was Portuguese, which is why there's no Spanish surname," Louisa continued. "Oh wait. There's more in this email. In 1870, it looks like he wasn't married yet. Damn. Listen to this. He was in his late twenties and his net worth was close to twenty thousand dollars. That would be a lot for a man of that age now, but in the 1800s?"

"He must have been a man of power and status at a young age," Malory said. "No wonder he ended up in politics."

"Wait, there is still more in this e-mail." Louisa continued reading, and as she did, a strange paralysis came over her body. She tried to swallow, but found it difficult.

"Malory."

"What?"

"I can't move."

"Why not?"

"It's her."

"Give me that," Malory said, snatching the paper out of Louisa's hand and read it out loud.

1880 census, Fernando, Taos, NM

> *Anthony SILVA, age 38, General Merchant, born in MO, father born in Azores, Port., mother born in AL.*

Emiliana, SILVA, wife, age 40. Self and parents born in NM

Sofia SILVA, daughter, age 16. At school, born in NM

Adelina Martinez, other, age 10. At school, self and parents born in NM

"Adelina Martinez: other. She was living in his home, just like you said she was," said Malory with awe.

"Martina, or something sounding like it, was a part of her name," said Louisa. "It's her." Her hands were shaking as Malory handed the sheet of paper back to her.

"You mean 'it's you.' Two names verified historically, Louisa," said Malory. "Two names!"

* * * *

Louisa needed more information and was determined to get it. She went to the state Historical Society which served as the library for genealogy in the state. She searched census records for 1870, 1880, 1890, most of which were destroyed in a fire, and 1900. She learned that during that time, Silva had two wives; an Emiliana after 1870, as listed in the 1880 census, and a Libby thereafter.

She then focused on Adelina. She went back to the 1910 census and found her in Ojo Caliente. "Adelina Martinez." Under employment it read "washwoman at the springs."

In the 1920 census, there was an Adelina Martinez, 50 years old. Under employment it read "at home." It appeared she never married. Louisa then searched the 1930 census and there was no listing for her. She determined Adelina had likely passed away and would research New Mexico death records to try and find her.

As Louisa put the pieces together, she realized a story was being revealed to her. It was Adelina's story, and she was being made privy to it.

Adelina

18

Adelina crawled over to the clean bedding spread across the floor. She lay back, her dark hair and gown drenched with sweat and her legs covered in blood.

She was alone when her water broke. She had walked the dirt path to the small house the evening before, wishing Antonio was in town. But he was in Washington and had been for several weeks. If he had been home would he have been with her? She had convinced herself that he would someday marry her and they would live as a family with their children. Such fantasies occupied her thoughts much of the time, just as they did that night when she gazed at the fire until she fell asleep. At dawn she woke to the feeling of warm water soaking her gown.

The *curandera* wiped one of the newborns clean and rubbed him with salt, a tradition long ago handed down by the Jewish midwives in Northern New Mexico. She handed him to Adelina and helped put him to her breast. Exhausted and overwhelmed, tears streamed down her cheeks. The *curandera* unwrapped the baby girl and cleaned her as she had the other.

"Dos bebito!"

Adelina nodded, still in a daze. As the baby nursed, she felt a contraction and let out a moan. Panicked, she looked to the *curandera* for help.

"Shhhh. Drink," the woman said, and handed her a tea made from creeping milkweed. "This is good for you."

Adelina took a sip of the tea and looked at the baby girl in the *curandera's* arms. She had Antonio's mouth. Wouldn't he be so proud of his children? She felt a swell of emotion. She had been so alone for so long and she would never be alone again.

Adelina's days and nights ran together as she cared for the two infants and a month quickly passed. She had not yet returned to the servant's quarters of Antonio's house and wouldn't until she was told to.

The day was sunny and mild and she swept the loose dirt on the packed floor out the open door. The river rushed in the distance, but she heard something else. Was someone coming on a horse? She smiled to herself as she thought it was Antonio.

As the sound grew closer, she realized there was more than one horse approaching, and fear shot through her body. Antonio always came alone. She stepped off the porch and walked briskly toward the road to better see in the distance. It was Antonio and behind him was his brother.

She walked toward them, shoulders back and head high.

"What are you doing here?" she asked Antonio as he brought his horse to a stop.

He said nothing and his silence frightened her. He climbed down and walked past her as the other man brought his horse to a stop.

"What are you doing here? I haven't seen you in months. Answer me," she said forcefully, grabbing his arm as he stepped onto the porch.

He pried her hand loose and continued to walk into the house, not looking at her. Adelina began to panic and forced herself past him and toward the babies, now asleep. She turned to face Antonio and told him to leave, but he shoved her aside, knocking her to the floor, and picked up one of the infants. The other man, right behind him, picked up the other, and the two men quickly walked out of the house. Adelina scrambled after them, crying in desperation.

"You can't keep them, Adelina," Antonio said firmly. "You are not married and must work. Who will care for them when you are away?"

for her. But this time no warm greetings were exchanged. Instead, the heated continuation of an earlier discussion continued.

"Stop talking about this nonsense," he said firmly.

"There's no place for us here," she said. "I want to go back to my family."

"I won't let you take her. Besides, there is no place for you with your family, I have told you that. No one wants you."

"How can you expect me to stay here, treated the way I am? The way people look at me and whisper behind my back. I am my daughter's nanny, not her mother. I am nothing to anyone but your mistress."

"Don't use that tone," he said, stepping closer so he could stand over her. "You have forgotten your place."

"We are leaving," she said.

"And where do you think you will go? What man will have you? You're soiled. You gave birth to two illegitimate children. You couldn't even marry in the church. I have provided for you since you were a child. How would you take care of yourself?"

Her dark eyes gleamed with anger. There was nothing more to say and she turned to walk away.

"I forbid it," he said, grabbing her arm and taking the child he too was so fond of out of her arms. "Don't challenge me, Adelina."

In that moment, she felt how powerless she really was. He was right. No one else would have her and there was no place for her to go. She was trapped. Tears filled her eyes as she watched him storm away, carrying their child. She knew she could never leave, not as long as her baby was here. As the last rays of sunlight filled the sky, she wrapped her shawl tightly around her shoulders and made her way back to the plaza of Ojo Caliente.

Later that night, as the full moon filtered through the small window, Adelina opened her eyes and she sat up suddenly, gasping. She looked around the small room, getting her bearings. As she recalled the fragments from her dream, her heart raced and she broke into a cold sweat.

In her dream, Auristella was next to a body of water and she walked in until her head was covered. With eyes closed and the stillness of no breath, her body became flimsy and floated deeper into the water, much the way a leaf might fall from side to side as it drifts to the ground. Tears filled Adelina's eyes and she felt the profound sadness of losing what was most precious to her. She closed her eyes and cried herself to sleep.

It was a month later that Auristella came down with the fever. Antonio was gone when she fell ill, but Adelina was there as her daughter slipped from this world into another, much like the leaf floating in her dream; drifting in and out of consciousness until she never came back.

* * * *

Louisa

Journal Entry

April 6, 2003

Malory and I leave for New Mexico this week. I'm amazed about finding Adelina Martinez, Antonio Silva, and the terraced gardens, and I wonder if it's possible that any more of my dreams or "knowing" could possibly be verified. It may be too much to expect, but I want to take this research trip anyway.

The emergence of Ma-Wi-Taa is no surprise. I'll call her that since it is the only name given to me. I felt something behind my right shoulder one day as I drove home from the grocery store. The energy of that presence sent an electric charge up and down my spine and I found myself turning to look in the back seat to make sure no one was there. Her presence is strong and independent, quite a dichotomy from Adelina who feels alone and bitter, yet somehow I relate to the energetic vibration of both these women.

In moments of self examination I continue to recognize the parallels between myself and Adelina. Perhaps I should restate that, I recognize the parallels in perception which in turn creates how I view my reality. Patterns in my relationships, my marriage, and life choices are staring back at me, revealing the depth of the dynamics I participate in. Perhaps my recognition, in the spirit of simultaneous lives having the ability to impact one another in that "moment," could in turn strengthen Adelina.

But it feels like the wind is stirring as Ma-Wi-Taa moves through me. There is an awakening of parts of me that have grown quiet over the years and I see that I too am a dichotomy. This is the human predicament; recognizing the conflicting aspects of self and realizing that perhaps we have a choice in which aspects we fuel.

Ma-Wi-Taa and Adelina; they are making me face myself in a way not otherwise possible.

19

They left before dawn and it was late afternoon when they pulled out of the parking lot of the grocery store in Santa Fe. "Okay," said Malory. "Since we're here, maybe you should tell me your plan."

"Well, I started a notebook," Louisa said as she shifted in the passenger seat to face Malory.

"Good idea."

"In it I have all the notes I've taken over the past few months from the census research, the information I gathered on the early Tewa Indians, Posi and Hupobi, and some historical information on Ojo. I also have my dream documentation. It's all together."

"And have you decided what we're going to be doing while we're there? Besides soaking in the springs and getting spa treatments, that is," Malory asked with a smile.

"I scheduled our massages and plan on doing lots of soaking. Aside from that, I have a list. I want to make a trip back into Santa Fe while we're here because I contacted the Chavez Library and they have some information on Silva, but they're not open right now." Louisa reached in the backseat for her back pack and pulled out a plastic bag. "Want some beef jerky?"

"Sure," said Malory, taking a piece from the bag that Louisa held open. "What kind of information does the library have?"

"The librarian said she had old photographs I could have copies of, as well as some articles. I also want to go to the graveyard in Santa Fe where Silva is buried, especially after that dream I had."

"There you go again, not keeping me informed. What dream?"

"I'm trying to remember when I had it. I think it was a few weeks ago." Louisa pulled out a water bottle, took a sip, and handed it to Malory. "I woke up from an Ojo dream with an image of a small headstone in my mind. I wrote 'something about a grave' in my notes. So I want to go by. Aside from that, I want to visit the Ojo Caliente graveyard to see if we can find Adelina Martinez.

"We can do that. Anything else?" she asked, handing the water bottle back to Louisa.

"The hike to Posi. I still don't know exactly how to get to Hupobi, though I know it's right there."

"Sounds like it's going to be a busy trip."

"But relaxing at the same time," Louisa said. "Or at least I hope it is. Oh my gosh— get over in the turn lane, Mal! The graveyard where Silva is buried is on this street."

"It is? Wait, I can see the graveyard from here," Malory said excitedly, pointing to the west. "We've been driving past it all this time and had no idea."

"We can go ahead and get this accomplished, then scratch it off the list," said Louisa.

"Always the task-master, but I love you for it."

"It's the only way I can get everything done. Okay," said Louisa, "here's the entrance."

As they spoke, their banter became more and more rapid as it generally did when they were excited, and it seemed their adventure was about to start. Malory turned the car onto the gravel drive of a well maintained graveyard. They saw a small covered structure with a book on a podium and stopped. Louisa hopped out of the car, found the location of Silva's grave, and ran back to the car. "I feel nervous" she said, shutting the car door, "but I'm not sure why."

"Because you're visiting the physical grave of a man whose spirit you sensed in the room that 'you' were intimately involved with. Not to mention a relationship that has followed you through space and time and created great havoc in your present life. Think about it. This is one of Matthew's other selves buried here in this graveyard," Malory said with much matter of fact enthusiasm.

"I guess that would be reason enough," Louisa said as she pulled her hair up into a pony tail and fidgeted nervously.

"I'd say it's reason enough, and I love it!" Malory exclaimed. "Oh, here we are. I'm taking pictures of this." Malory grabbed her camera and they both got out of the car. "This head-stone looks pretty new. It must have been replaced since 1910."

Louisa nodded and walked past Malory and Silva's headstone, pulled like a magnet to the small grave behind his. She knelt down in front of the tombstone and ran her fingers across the weathered lettering. Her head began to spin and goose-bumps covered her arms and legs. "This says Auristella Silva. Born in 1886 and died in 1891," she said under her breath. She backed away from the grave and walked as fast as she could back to the car. She pulled out her notebook and frantically flipped through the pages. Then she saw it: the picture of the small house she had drawn after her dream. She read through her notes as fast as she could. *There were two children- one lived and the other died.*

Malory walked over to the car holding the camera. "Is everything okay?"

Louisa looked up at her from where she sat in the passenger seat, paper spread across the dash board. "Oh my gosh. Malory. Do you remember the dream I had about the two baby beds, and how there were two children not one, but that one died?"

Malory nodded.

"Follow me," said Louisa.

The two walked back over to the gravesite. "This little girl was born in 1886," said Malory. "Louisa? What does your gut tell you? It's gotten you this far…"

Not answering and reeling in her own thoughts, Louisa responded with more questions. "Were they twins? Did she just get pregnant right away?"

"Louisa, what's your feeling?"

"This is the child that died in my dream. And that she and her brother were born to Adelina in 1886. Maybe twins. Maybe one after the other, but she was the mother of both." Louisa knelt down and ran her fingers across the engraving again.

"Didn't Antonio's brother have someone living in his home that was born in 1886?" asked Malory. "That would have been consistent with your dream that a child went to Antonio's brother."

Louisa nodded. "But why would he give his child away?"

"Well," said Malory, "wasn't that the only child in his brother's home as far as we could tell from the census data?"

"I think so. Why?"

"In many cultures and in past times, it was important that there always be an heir."

"That would make sense," said Louisa. From where she knelt on the ground, she looked up at the sky.

"I can't believe it," said Malory. "You found her. I take that back-I can totally believe it. Nothing would surprise me at this point."

Malory held out her hand to Louisa who took it and stood up. They walked back to the car, loaded up, and drove slowly down the gravel drive to the main street. As they drove north toward Ojo Caliente, Louisa's focus was elsewhere.

"Mal, I feel like we could just turn around and go home now, like finding that grave and affirming what I dreamt was the whole point of coming here. What else could possibly happen?"

"Well, we're not going home and I wouldn't be so sure."

They drove in silence and Louisa's mind drifted. It could have been twenty minutes or two hours for all Louisa knew. She was in the car but not. She could feel herself floating, similar to breathing happy gas at the dentist. But she was yanked back to reality when she started to choke and found her breathing strained, her heart racing. She looked up and saw the large mesa as they passed over the river. *What is this about?* She took a deep breath and glanced over at Malory, whose look back indicated she knew what Louisa was thinking.

"You better hang on," Malory said with a suspecting smile. "Something tells me more is coming."

They soon approached the town of Ojo Caliente and turned toward the springs. Now becoming familiar, the tires made a crunching sound as they pulled into the unpaved parking lot. When Louisa got out of the car, her legs were weak and wobbly beneath her and ached like she had run a marathon the day before. She knew if it was possible, she had energetically been doing just that.

20

The two sat at the same kitchen table they had three months earlier in the small house they would call home for the next few days. On the wall behind them table was a collage of old black and white photographs taken from the area, haphazardly stuck in a frame. Malory sat across from Louisa drinking a diet coke, studying the collage and guessing what year each photo was taken. Louisa pulled out her notes to get a sense of the cast of players again, particularly since she had found Auristella's grave.

"I wish we had a big board so we could make a flow chart," Malory said, pulling a loaf of artesian bread out of a brown paper bag.

"You can make one out of paper towels if you want," said Louisa, studying her notes. Malory handed her a hunk of buttered bread which she absently took and started to eat.

"The pencil would only tear a paper towel flow chart," Malory said. "What are you looking at?"

"New Mexico death records for 'Martinez.' They have deaths after 1900 on the internet. The site warned that it was common for a letter or two to be incorrect in the names, or for the age of the deceased to be off by a year or so. They list the name, year, and county. There are a few I think could be her, but none are in Taos County."

"Don't you remember that website you found addressed changes in county lines?" Malory asked. "Taos and Rio Arriba counties pretty much divide this area. Are there any for Rio Arriba county?"

Louisa looked at the records. "There's an Abelina Martinez that died in Rio Arriba County, and if I do the math, this person is around the age at which Adelina probably died."

"Well, she didn't have any family Louisa. It's likely her name could have been entered incorrectly."

"That probably means she's buried in an unmarked grave. Let's still check out the graveyard, though. We can do that in the morning." Louisa pushed her paperwork to the side. "Let's go play."

Leaving their work where it was, they went over to the springs. It was a clear night and Louisa and Malory had the good fortune of being the only ones in the Cliffside springs. The two were in the middle of a quiet conversation, when a very fit, bald guy, wearing a thong bikini bathing suit no less, came walking briskly toward the pool and, bypassing the stone stairs, stepped in off the side. He pushed through the water to Louisa and Malory, until he was right in front of them.

"Hi!" he said enthusiastically.

"Hi," said Louisa and Malory in unison.

"I've been mountain bike riding on the trails all afternoon, and boy, these springs feel great," he said. "So where are you two from?"

"Oklahoma," said Louisa.

"You girls here on vacation?"

"You could say that," said Malory. "It's a working vacation."

Louisa nodded and smiled. "So are you from around here?"

"Not originally, but I live in Santa Fe now," he said.

"What do you do?" asked Louisa.

"Engineer during the day. You guys?"

"I'm a social worker and run a small non-profit," said Louisa.

"I'm a stay-at-home mom," said Malory.

"Well alright," he said.

A small group approached the pool, put down their towels and got in the water. The conversation quickly turned political and Louisa listened as Malory found herself surrounded by other conspiracy theorists such as herself. She casually pulled away from the group and sat quietly, looking up at the cliffs.

The fit and friendly bald guy came over and sat next to her. "Have you ever had Watsu before?" he asked her.

"Watsu... is that the bodywork that is done in the water?" she asked.

"Yeah. Have you ever had it done?"

"No, I can't say I have."

"Do you want to?"

"Um, I don't know."

"Do you want me to do it to you?" he asked.

Louisa looked toward Malory, trying to get her attention. "I thought you said you were some type of engineer."

"I am. I just do this as a hobby. Come on. You'll love it," he said, pulling her into the middle of the pool.

"Oh, that's okay, really, you don't have to," Louisa said, trying to get out of it, but before she knew it, she was on her back in the water, supported by only his hand under the small of her back. She couldn't tell what was happening as he manipulated her limbs, but at one point she suspected her leg was wrapped around his neck. She didn't open her eyes because she didn't really want to know.

After what seemed like an eternity, he pulled her body over to a small waterfall where water flowed into the pool and carefully put her head under it. She opened her eyes.

"What do you think?" he asked.

"Wow. Thanks." She still didn't believe he was legitimate. He thanked her for letting him work on her and started talking to someone else.

Malory came over, laughing. "You did really well with that. You know, trusting this stranger to have control of your body in the water."

"How did I get myself into that? I somehow managed to escape peer pressure my entire youth, yet in my thirties I couldn't say no to Watsu? What does that say about me? And why didn't you help me?"

"I don't know," she said, giggling. "I guess I wanted to see how it would all unfold. Your leg—it was wrapped around his neck."

"Hey, now it's your turn," said the Watsu-engineer as he approached them from behind. He took Malory's arm and pulled her toward the center of the pool.

"Enjoy," Louisa said and climbed out of the pool, grabbed her towel, and looked until she found a pool that was empty. Against the starry sky were dark masses that by day were sand colored cliffs. The warm water encapsulated her body and she closed her eyes, absorbing the silence.

She replayed snapshots of the previous few months leading to finding the child's grave, and how when she saw the tombstone, she felt a recognition that shot through every fiber of her being. It was her child. Just as Isaac and Caleb were to her, the little girl was to Adelina. A knot formed in her throat and tears swelled in her eyes.

She heard footsteps behind her and Louisa turned to see Malory as she stepped into the spring.

"Can I join you?"

"Of course," Louisa answered quietly.

"Taking it all in?" Malory asked, looking up at the stars.

"I'm trying to."

"Are you okay, sweetie?"

Louisa nodded. "Thanks, Malory." She turned back to the stars, and with each breath she fell further inward. This was how it was supposed to be: the warmth of the water, the cliffs, the sky, the breeze, and the ebb and flow of Spirit as it touched her psyche. This was an Ojo state of mind.

* * * *

Malory stood at the counter in front of the coffee pot when Louisa wandered into the kitchen. "Good morning sleepy head," she said, pouring a cup of coffee.

"What time is it?" asked Louisa, sitting down at the table.

"It's nine o'clock. I got up about fifteen minutes ago."

"I never sleep this late. For that matter, I slept better than I've ever slept here before."

"Maybe it was the Watsu—I slept great too," said Malory.

"I think I might need it every night if it works that well," said Louisa. Malory smiled and handed Louisa a mug. "You made me tea? You take such good care of me."

"We take good care of each other," said Malory.

Louisa took a sip. "You know what they say: the men will come and go, but you'll always have your female friends."

"The scary thing is that there is probably some real truth to that," Malory said with raised eyebrows. "So what's it going to be this morning?"

"Graveyard."

After a quick breakfast, they hopped in the car. "I need to get more film," said Malory. "Let's stop at the little shop up the road."

Louisa pulled up in front of a small building with a sign that said "The Mercantile" and they walked in the front doors. Malory went to look for film and Louisa looked at the various clothing and other items on display. She meandered into a small side room where she saw a bookshelf and a rack of postcards, one of which was a black and white photograph of several men and was labeled "The Mercantile." She looked at the etched ceiling tiles in the picture and then at the tiles in the shop—they were the same. In that moment, she realized she was in the original building that was Antonio's business. The realization caused her to feel a lump in her throat. She then looked down at the bookshelf again and saw an informally bound book. She flipped through the pages and saw it was about the history of Ojo Caliente. She walked to the front of the shop and asked the woman behind the counter, "Is this for sale?"

"No. That was written and sold to raise money for a new roof for the church. But you know what? The man who wrote it, our local historian, lives right behind the Mercantile. If you have a few minutes I bet he'd come over and talk to you about it."

"Malory, do we have time?" Louisa asked Malory, who was now walking to the counter.

"Of course we do. Let's give him a call," she said with a nod.

For more than an hour they sat as the old man told them what he knew and tried to answer Louisa's questions.

"Silva worked with a man named Miguel Martinez to acquire the land," he said. "People were told their families could stay forever, but if they signed over their deeds, Silva would pay them. When he had the majority of the deeds, he then owned the common lands, which held the springs. That was what he really wanted. The locals hated him for swindling them. The land's still not under clear title, not only because of the way it was transferred originally, but later sold. Anthony Jr. took over after his father died and ran everything into the ground. Silva has a great grandson who is still alive and he could challenge ownership."

"Is this great grandson related through Anthony Jr.?" Louisa asked.

"No, no," he responded. "Sometime in the early 1900s, Silva had an affair with a cousin of mine," he said. Louisa's heart sank as she thought of Adelina. "My cousin was much younger than him," he continued. "She had two children by him. He never did anything to take care of her, but they had his name. That Silva— he was a scrounger."

When it was time for them to get moving, Louisa and Malory walked back out to the car. "That son of a bitch," Louisa said angrily. "He just dumped Adelina after fifteen years? From best I can tell she had no one but him and he contributed to it being that way. He took her kids and then left her for someone else. I can't begin to express my negative feelings about this."

"Well," Malory said, "Jerry said it all. 'That Silva—he was a scrounger.'"

"And boy, did she love him in spite of it. What's the deal with these men who are never exposed to the aftermath of their decisions or held accountable for their actions?" Louisa asked with contempt as she put on her seatbelt and started the ignition. "It really pisses me off."

"I can tell. Is it possible you're talking about more than Antonio?"

"Is it that obvious?" asked Louisa with a guilty smile. "It's just— Matthew! He takes no responsibility and sees nothing wrong with treating someone he loved as if they were disposable all those years." She backed the car away from the Mercantile and pulled out onto the road. "Poor Adelina."

"There's definitely a karmic pattern. And Adelina probably didn't feel like she had much choice," said Malory, snapping the camera closed after loading the film.

"No, she was the Hispanic servant and mistress to the man who apparently owned the town, but she was in love with him." Louisa pulled up to the stop sign at the main highway. "For heaven's sake, the graveyard's right here? We could have walked!"

"Right under our noses and we never even noticed it," Malory replied.

Louisa turned onto the dirt road that led to the back of the cemetery and they got out of the car. As she walked through the oldest section, she noticed it had been somewhat undisturbed for quite some time; the ground was covered with a prickly brush and strewn with broken wooded crosses. The now unmarked graves were only obvious by the remaining mound of cracked soil— the only clue that there was once a burial there.

Malory strolled with her camera in hand and ended up on the opposite side of the cemetery. "Louisa, I think you need to be over here," she gestured with a wide sweeping motion.

Louisa walked toward Malory, reading the years marked on each headstone. "They seem to be in order," she said. "I guess people didn't buy burial plots back then. See Malory? This one is 1920, here's a 1924, and then a few from 1925, and so on. Did you see these metal nameplates stuck in the ground? They are totally rusted over, but I think they have names written on them. This is a mess."

"Let's just keep looking," said Malory.

Louisa made her way around some particularly dense brush, trying to look at a metal nameplate that was lying on the ground. As she took a step, she landed on the ground with a thud. "Oh my God!" she screamed and looked down to see the majority of her leg was underground. "Help me out!"

"Are you okay?" Malory asked, scrambling over and pulling Louisa up by the arm. "Jeez Louise, you fell into a grave!"

Louisa pulled her leg out of the ground and with Malory's help stood crouched over examining the small thorns and stickers that covered her socks and sweatpants. "I fell into a sinkhole over an unmarked grave? These things don't happen in real life—I'm freaking out. The disrespect of it—disturbing the dead!"

"Well, it must happen because it just did. And you don't believe any of that nonsense about disturbing the dead," said Malory, pulling thorns out of the seat of Louisa's pants. "They just didn't pack the dirt well back then."

"Maybe we should go back so I can change clothes," Louisa said, at that point "done" with the graveyard. They started to walk back to the car.

"Louisa, you don't generally believe in coincidence, right?"

"Not generally. You know that," said Louisa as she opened the car door and climbed in the driver's seat. Malory had a questioning look on her face.

Louisa returned her stare, took a deep breath, and nodded. They walked back to where Louisa fell. There were three unmarked graves in a row. She looked at what dates she could find and followed the row: 1925, 1926, and up to 1930. The beginning of the next row was beyond Adelina's death date, which from the death records looked to be 1929.

"So what if it's right here, but it's not specifically where I fell?"

"So you stepped into the grave next to it. What's your gut tell you?" Malory asked. "You knew their names. You knew relationships. You knew about a baby dying with the Silva name that wasn't listed in any census data."

"You know," Louisa said, kicking at a loose tumbleweed next to her, "the day I was at your house and I got the e-mail from the volunteer and found Adelina Martinez living in Silva's home, do you know what words popped into my mind? 'Never doubt yourself.' But as all this is unfolding, it seems unreal."

"I'm sure it feels weird, but from the outside, it is so evident that you are being led," said Malory, taking a picture of the hole left from Louisa's leg. "We'll label this 'where Louisa fell into a grave.'"

"Trusting these random things that come to me is hard. I could be making it all up," said Louisa.

"Sure. But you wouldn't have census data to back it up if you were. If we want to, we can find a rational explanation for any occurrence we can't explain. That's our conditioning," said Malory, stepping back to get a picture of Louisa standing in the graveyard.

"But then every belief system that acknowledges a greater power accepts there is more than the concrete and rational, right?" Louisa asked rhetorically.

"That would be the common denominator, yes."

"Well," said Louisa, "that statement should be clarified to state that as long as things are within certain parameters of what those belief systems deem to be acceptable."

"The Louisa I know doesn't worry about what's acceptable. Whatever's happening here is real. Trust yourself. What more affirmation do you need than what you've gotten?"

Louisa quietly nodded, noticing a cool breeze and sudden cloud cover. She walked over to a ridge and picked up two rocks.

"What are you doing?" asked Malory.

Louisa carried the rocks to the unmarked grave and placed them on the ground. She knelt down for a moment in silence. *"You are remembered."* She felt a rush of energy through her arms and legs and then a surge in her chest. A gust of wind blew across the graveyard and she looked up just as snow flakes started to touch the ground. With a silent thank you to Spirit, she turned and walked back to the car.

21

Their last morning in Ojo was sunny and crisp. Louisa and Malory got up early and after sitting by the fire drinking coffee, made their way over to the restaurant.

"Remember the last time we sat in this restaurant?" Malory asked, cutting her *huevos rancheros* with her fork. "You confidently told me the name of the woman who slept in the hammock sounded like 'Martina.' Can you believe it was only three months ago? Think about how much you know about her now! Not to mention the other dreams and the terraced gardens—who knows what more is coming."

"It's a cool story, don't you think?"

"Oh yeah," Malory said, sipping her coffee. "You need to be writing this all down."

"I am, here and there."

"So what's on the agenda for today?"

"Posi. Let's get going in case the weather turns again."

They walked out of the old hotel and down the wooden steps when Malory stopped. "Hey," she said, "before we put on our hiking shoes, let's go check out the old barn. The massage therapist who worked on me yesterday told me it was being restored."

"Let's do it later," said Louisa.

"No. Right now," said Malory, looking at Louisa firmly and pulling her arm. "I *really* think it's important you see this."

Louisa looked at her perplexed. "You're acting funny." Malory continued to pull her in the direction she wanted to go, so with an exasperated sigh, Louisa conceded.

They found the old dirt road that led to the barn, climbed over a locked gate, climbed through a fence and walked down the path. Louisa noticed it ran along the Rio Ojo and the landscape had changed dramatically. To her left were small mountains covered with piñon, large rock, and quartz of varying colors. On her right were cottonwoods that lined the river, their new leaves shimmering in the morning sun.

The two continued in silence for several minutes. The path began to curve, and as it did, large scraggly trees came into view. They seemed oddly familiar to Louisa, and as she got closer, part of the adobe barn came into view. The trees were behind the barn on the left. Her pace slowed as she stared at the trees and her heart began to beat rapidly. She knew those trees; from her repeated dreams about the barn that had been turned into a Bed & Breakfast. Her arms and legs began to feel weak and she could hear her heart pounding in her ears. As she climbed to the top of the small ridge, she saw it.

"Oh my God," she said under her breath. There it was in front of her—the house in her dream to the west of the barn. The house where the woman in her dream placed her feet on the cold, hard, dirt floor as she swung her legs out of the hammock. The house with the two baby beds—one small because the child had died. She looked at Malory and choked, "That's it."

"What's it?"

"The house."

"In your dreams?"

Louisa nodded, staring at the physicality of it. The old house had two front doors, like a motel, and a porch across the front. It was identical to the house by the barn in her dream. "I saw those big trees as we approached and I got goose bumps. I never would have believed I would see this house."

"Louisa, it's painted pink. You had a dream about a house that had pink walls in January. Do you remember that? And the barn that was turned into a B & B? This barn is being refurbished. Do you see? Do you see?" she asked with excitement. "And you think you can explain this away? I don't think so. Let's go get the camera. And I want to see the picture you drew of the house."

They trekked back to the house. Louisa pulled out her notebook and looked for the drawing.

"Is that it?" Malory asked as Louisa handed her the paper. "Oh. I'm almost speechless. That's it. It's unbelievable." Malory started to read aloud the dream written above the drawing. "'I am back in front of the barn. Same trees, same blue sky, same landscape. But what's to the left of the barn? I had to get closer. I finally see it. In front of me is a small adobe house. It has two exterior doors, almost next to each other, similar to a motel. There is a porch, supported by wooden posts across the front of the house, and a few trees blocking my view...' Louisa, your description of it is identical. It's amazing."

"It's like this whole trip was about that one dream," Louisa said, staring at the picture. "Knowing about her children—the grave, and finding the house. I have no words right now. I'm overwhelmed."

They got the camera, climbed the fences again, and walked back to the barn. Louisa walked over and stepped onto the broken planks that made up the porch to look in one of the front doors, but the roof of the house was falling in, making entry impossible. The windows gave a glimpse at the inside, but she knew no one could feel the emotion it held but her.

After taking pictures there was nothing there for them to do, but Louisa didn't want to leave. She took one last look to say goodbye and turned to leave. It was hard to walk away.

As they made their way back down the well-packed dirt road, tears streamed down Louisa's cheeks. It was irrational, inexplicable emotion, and she tried to hide it.

"I imagine you walked down this road more than a hundred times," Malory said.

Louisa closed her eyes and felt Adelina, and she knew with a degree of certainty unavailable to her before that she was real. And Malory was right; somewhere in another space and time, Adelina was on that very path walking to meet Antonio.

Adelina

22

Adelina walked up the path to the small adobe parish on the plaza of Ojo Caliente. The morning sun filtered through the leaves on the tall cottonwoods along the river, casting a mosaic of light on the packed dirt. The breeze grew stronger for an instant and the trees echoed the sound of a mother hushing her children.

When she approached the doorway she knelt, made the sign of the cross, and took her seat on the back pew. She reached around to rub her back, aching from long days bent over a washboard at the springs, and looked down at her lap as people filed in.

She heard Antonio's voice behind her. He was with his wife and son and he stopped next to her, quietly shaking the hand of another man. Without looking at Adelina, he touched his wife's back, guiding her down the aisle to the front of the church.

Bitterness rose in her chest and as others walked past without acknowledging her, she felt like an outcast. She watched Antonio from behind and pressed her lips tightly together.

When the mass was over, she quickly exited the church. Her skirt made a swishing noise with each brisk step as she tried to escape the rejection that had long ago taken root inside of her.

She heard the stomp of boots and turned to see one of Antonio's workers from the Mercantile running to catch up with her. "Antonio said meet him down the dirt path," he said, and then made his way back to the group that was milling in front of the church.

She observed the crowd from a distance and felt disdain. How had she grown so alienated and alone? Antonio stood among them, next to his suitable wife, making conversation and shaking hands. He locked eyes with Adelina and gave her a quick nod. She turned and walked down the road, across the bridge, and toward the small house.

Antonio slowly broke away from the crowd and followed Adelina. She waited several minutes before she saw him come up the path. The spring breeze blew a wisp of her hair out of its bun and she pulled it down, letting her hair fall down her back. As he approached, he put his arm around her waist, pulling her close. She held her breath, afraid to move past her anger. The warmth of his touch softened her and as she smelled his familiar scent, she let herself melt into his embrace.

When the sun was getting low, the two walked hand in hand along the river. Antonio looked over at Adelina and gave her hand a gentle squeeze.

"I miss you living in the servant's quarters," he said.

"I don't miss Libby."

Antonio nodded and recalled the day his wife told him she would leave and take their son back to the east coast if he didn't get his mistress out of their home. In the prime of his political career, he acquiesced.

"I'm leaving for Washington next week."

"But you just got back," said Adelina.

"I know, but I must."

Adelina looked to the ground as she walked, lost in thought. For more than ten years she had been his mistress and she found herself waiting, alone; a week, a month, maybe more, never knowing when he would appear. But he always did, eventually, and those moments kept her hanging on.

"I want to be your wife, not your mistress."

"Adelina, please."

"You tell me you love me."

"And how would that look?" he asked in a slightly condescending tone. "You are Hispano—uneducated and of a different class. It wouldn't help my reelection."

"So I am not worthy of you? After giving birth to two children and loving you for all these years?"

Antonio stopped walking and turned to face her. "No one understands our love but us. Don't you know that?"

Adelina nodded quietly. Antonio brushed the loose hair away from her eyes and kissed her gently on the mouth. "Have I not always taken care of you?" he asked.

She nodded again, wanting to say the things she never had the courage to say. She wasn't good enough for him, but he had been seeing her for more than a decade. She wanted a family of her own, but he took their children away from her. She was his mistress, and no one else in town would have her. But she didn't speak.

They walked to the end of the dirt path. "Go to the mercantile tomorrow and get what you need," he said. "I must go. I am expected."

"When will I see you again?" she asked.

"Soon. Very soon."

Louisa

23

The kids were on the couch in the living room watching TV while Alan sat in the bedroom, mindlessly surfing the net. But he was only pretending he was mindless; the reality was he was providing himself a distraction from his festering irritation. Louisa had just called. She was on her way back from Ojo and said she'd be home in thirty minutes. She sounded so excited to see the kids and happy to hear his voice, so why was he filled with contempt?

He fidgeted in the chair, chewing on his ring finger—an odd nervous habit he'd had since he was a kid. "Daddy?" he heard from the living room.

"Your mom will be home in a few minutes," he called. And he meant it. She could take over. After all, she was selfish enough to leave, right? The bitch goes running off to chase after some spirit voodoo—so she'll have to deal with everything from that point forward.

He caught himself; he knew his rage toward her was not completely rational. He knew that the very qualities that led her on a crazy research trip were what drew him to her in the first place. She was a great mom, he'd give her that, and she somehow managed to juggle her career and the kids in a remarkable way. He knew she would, which was why he knew she'd be the mother of his children. He relied on her heavily—she kept things in order and his feet on the ground. But in that moment, he hated her. She went off and left him to take care of the kids. He even spent Saturday afternoon at a birthday party. What was he, a fucking woman?

The dogs started barking and he suspected they heard the garage door opening. In a few minutes he heard the door in the utility room close.

"Hi guys!" Louisa called.

"Mommy's home!" yelled the boys, running to greet her.

"I sure did miss you. Where's Daddy?"

"He's on the 'puter,'" said Caleb.

"Okay. Let me go tell him I'm home."

Alan heard her enter the room.

"Hi honey," she said, leaning down to give him a kiss. He didn't look up, so she kissed his forehead. "I can't wait to tell you about my research trip. It was unbelievable!" He glanced up and then went back to what he was doing.

"Are you not going to say hello?" she asked. He gave no response.

He felt her stiffen behind his chair. "Okay then, I guess I'll go get started on dinner."

"We do fine without you," he said in a snide tone as she started to walk out of the bedroom.

"Excuse me?" she asked, shocked.

Alan didn't respond. He just stared at the monitor, jaw clenched, until he heard her leave the room.

Louisa took the boys' hands and led them to the kitchen. "That grouchy Daddy," she said. "He must have had a bad day."

She let go of their little hands and picked up a dirty sock, a Frisbee, a sippy cup and a pair of Caleb's dirty sweatpants as she made her way through the house.

"How about we eat a big bowl of fruit?" Louisa asked, opening the refrigerator only to see it was empty. Not just sort of empty, but nothing in it but expired milk and condiments empty.

"Alan?" she called. "Did you go to the store like you said you would? There isn't anything to feed the kids."

"That's your job!" he yelled back.

She stared into the refrigerator and fought back her tears. Clearly she was going to be punished for leaving. She put on a smile for the boys, closed the door and asked, "Who wants to go to the store with Mommy?"

* * * *

Many a book has been written about creating your own reality. Louisa had seen them, and she'd even read a few. They could mostly be found in the New Age section of the bookstore, but in "reality," it wasn't a new concept at all. In fact, Louisa found a book about the very subject matter written in 1907 that quoted biblical scriptures as its validation. It seemed to be that way with these "New Age" ideas—most of them weren't new at all.

Regardless of its foundation, Louisa knew she needed to look at the concept in a new light. Sure, most people were concerned with manifesting money or a soul mate, but considering everything Louisa had been going through, there had to be more to it than that. Do we eventually have to acknowledge that maybe "we" are manifesting on a level that is far greater than what we think about? The ability to create our own realities was a great idea to play with, but if we accept that we do it, doesn't that mean we have to take full responsibility for the very fabric of our lives? That's what Louisa struggled with, since there seemed to be some real flaws in her fabric.

She could start with the way she had always felt cast aside growing up, or the issues with abandonment she was so ready to be finished with. She kind of felt like a victim the day she got home from her research trip and Alan was so hateful. She also felt like a victim to Matthew's promiscuous and indifferent ways when they were young. Adelina clearly had a lot of baggage with Antonio, and the woman who was drowned was a victim in the most basic of ways. But if we create our own realities, she was beginning to realize, those elements of human experience must have some validity to reaching higher understanding or they wouldn't be manifested, right? Or she could only hope…

She would have delved further into those ideas upon her return from New Mexico, along with trying to assimilate the almost unbelievable nature of her trip, but the night of her arrival home marked the beginning of a whole different form of manifestation not yet discussed. It was that night that she first found herself draped over the toilet, praying the intense nausea would pass.

It didn't. Instead it grew more and more perpetual and a month later she was ten pounds lighter and living on the bathroom floor.

"What did the doctor say?" Alan asked from the bathroom doorway. He was covered in sweat and in his bike garb. He had opted out of going with her for the CAT scan that morning.

"My gallbladder isn't functioning. They're going to try and get me in for surgery in a few days to have it removed. And there's some kind of tumor in my liver."

Alan's expression softened. He walked over to Louisa and pulled her up off the floor. "Are the kids asleep?"

Louisa nodded.

"Do you want to sit outside with me while I have a glass of wine?" he asked.

He had practically ignored her for weeks and he chose now to bond? "For a little while," she said.

She followed him out to the patio where they sat side by side with little conversation. The sky was almost dark and Louisa watched a small bat fly in and out of the trees.

"Is God trying to teach me a lesson that I haven't treated you or taken care of you like I should have by taking you away?" asked Alan.

"I don't know that I'm willing to be a martyr for that cause," Louisa said. "Let's don't go there unless we have to."

"I haven't been there for you lately," said Alan, looking up at the sky.

"No, you haven't. Marriage has been hard on us."

"I'm sorry," he said and took her hand. "I'll try and do better."

The two went back inside. Alan made his way to the computer and Louisa to the kitchen where she loaded the dishwasher and wiped down the counters. When she was finished, she went back and ran a hot bath. After a long soak, she brushed her teeth, put on her jammies and pulled down the covers to get into bed.

"Weezie!" Alan called from the office.

Louisa hurried to the office. "Are you crazy!" she said. "You're going to wake up the kids."

"I did a little research," he said as she walked in the room. "According to Chinese Medicine, the gallbladder holds victimization."

"Wow." Her thoughts turned to Adelina and the girl who was drowned. "What possessed you to research that?" she asked.

"I just wondered what you were manifesting."

Before they could discuss it, the phone rang, and Louisa went to answer it.

"Hey sweetie. How are you?" It was Malory.

"Hanging in there," said Louisa. "I'm probably going in on June fifth to get this horrible organ taken out."

"Oh my God, that's in a few days," said Malory. "Listen, I wanted to tell you I went to the website of a medical intuitive. According to what I read, the gallbladder holds abandonment and victimization."

"Did you talk to Alan?" Louisa asked, perplexed.

"No. Why?"

"He just did some research about what the gallbladder holds energetically."

"You're kidding," said Malory. "I'm impressed, and surprised."

"You guys are freaking me out," said Louisa.

"Sounds like you're going to have to lose an organ to heal."

"I hope I don't make a habit of that. With all my baggage, there won't be anything left," said Louisa sarcastically. "I know, let's call this the 'Big Purge'."

"I love it!" said Malory. "I'm glad to hear that you still have your sense of humor. And June fifth is just around the corner."

A week later, Louisa lay in bed resting when the phone rang. It was a week after her surgery. Both the dogs were curled up against her legs and the cat was on her stomach. She grabbed the nightstand to pull herself up while the animals tried desperately to remain in place. The cat finally jumped to the floor and Louisa reached for the phone but missed the call.

Since she went to all that effort to sit up, she went ahead and got out of bed. She went to her computer to check e-mail and then decided to read her astrological forecast. Her horoscope addressed the fact that Saturn had slowly, over the course of two years, moved through her sign (Gemini) since the spring of 2001.

"This planet influences dealing with karma and past lives," she read. She rethought the past year and a half of her life and wasn't surprised. Alan had given her the gift of going to Ojo at the end of 2001. And when did Saturn pass out of her sign? June fifth.

Louisa went outside and walked down the steps so her feet could be on the grass. She looked up at the trees and then the June sky and closed her eyes. In that moment she hoped that she did, in fact, purge what appeared to be a pattern of abandonment and victimization, and that with the recognition of those patterns, there was a release that cut across space and time.

Ma-Wi-Taa

24

She rose out of sleep, and felt her head heavy as it hung toward her chest. As she opened her eyes, the events of the day before came back to her; the cave, her instructions, and being spotted by the men. She cautiously opened her eyes. The sky had a purple hue as the sun began its journey above the mountains. She was on the ground with her back against a tree, her arms tied behind her. Nightfall had come shortly after she was captured. She was walked down to the camp and questioned by the one that tied the ropes around her. He was rough and harsh and grabbed her by her hair as he quietly whispered threats, only bits and pieces of which she could understand. He pushed her against the remains of the pueblo wall, grabbing at the waist of his pants and forcing himself on her. Were it not for one of the others pulling him off, she would have been raped. His smell fresh on her clothes, she sat awake most of the night, scared to sleep.

A man appeared in a doorway— the one who walked her down after she was caught and who prevented her from being raped the night before. He spoke to her in Spanish, only some of which she understood from childhood, but she dared not respond. Starting a fire close to where she was sitting, he knelt beside her and offered her water from a chipped pot. She looked down and stared at the ground.

"I'm surprised to see a young woman out alone," he said. "You must have had a reason."

She held her gaze on the ground. "You may not realize this," he continued, "but I am the closest thing to a friend you have here. These other men, they will use you for whatever they wish." He threw another dead branch on the small fire as he studied her.

He was a soldier for the Spanish army. He heard about the revolt in Nuevo Mexico thirteen years earlier and was impressed with the resolve of the native people. He was twenty at the time and had traveled with his family from Spain to the colony of Mexico. Following the rumors of great wealth, he made his way to El Paso, at which time he learned of the uprising and that there was no gold. Only a worthless blue stone the native people considered precious but was worth nothing. His gaze shifted to the turquoise pendant she wore around her neck.

The Spanish, including the ones he camped with, felt disdain for and superior to the natives, which was why he feared for the young woman before him. That was the reality of war; women were taken as property, children were taken from their families, and people were killed for fighting for their homes. But at some point over the past nine months, he had lost his passion for the cause of taking back Nuevo Mexico for the Crown of Spain. He found himself struggling with the unthinkable: what right did they have to force these people to live a different way of life? It was a moral dilemma not allowed for within his position as a soldier, but one he was having nonetheless.

Pulling his eyes way from the blue pendant she was wearing, his gaze moved upward to her face. Her black hair was in a braid down her back, and as he studied her face, he noticed a birthmark across her cheek. He found himself staring into her dark eyes for just a moment before she quickly looked away. He walked over and untied her from the tree, grabbed his gun and extra ammunition, and led her toward his horse. Her hands still tied behind her back, he pulled her foot into a stirrup and pushed her up. Untying the reins, he silently led the horse away from the camp just as the sky brightened to shades of blue.

They walked until the sun was well into the sky then stopped along a stream where he filled his canteen with water. Her hands were still tied, but she thought maybe she could run. She didn't know where they were going or what was happening. He removed his stiletto from his belt and reached up to cut the cords that bound her wrists. He took her arm and guided her off the horse.

Stepping down, she stood quietly, afraid of what might come next. She slowly held up the water pouch she wore around her waist, as if to ask permission to fill it. Taking it from her, he knelt down, dunked it in the stream and handed it back. She kept her eyes on the ground. Now was the time to get away, to run. Or had he set her free? She was expected back at the cave by high sun that day. She would never make it by then, but if she tried to run away, she may never make it at all.

Gesturing for her to get back on the horse, he climbed up first and then offered her a hand. Kicking his heels into its flanks, the animal took off in a gallop and they headed north, toward her home.

* * * *

They rode together at an easy pace in silence and he wondered what his comrades thought after waking to discover both he and their captive missing. There was a fair chance they would come looking for them. That was, after all, why they had been sent back east; to survey the status of the refugees and report back what they knew. It seemed it was only a matter of time before the Spanish overpowered the Indians and took back control of the colony, but it had proven far more difficult than they had anticipated.

Ma-Wi-Taa sat behind the soldier and her mind ran through her options. If she jumped off and ran, he might shoot her. If she stayed with him until nightfall, she could sneak away while he slept. Yes, that was what she would do.

The summer sun beat down and they stopped to take a break beneath a boulder that provided not only shade, but a place to remain out of view. No words had been spoken since that morning and she cautiously observed him as he looked out over the terrain with a look of deep thought in his eyes. Perhaps he was as confused about what to do from there as she was. Leaning back against the rock, her eyes grew heavy, and she drifted into sleep.

She woke with a jump. Had she heard a gunshot? She was alone and the sun was beginning its journey toward the western peaks. Stepping out from beneath the boulder, she looked and saw that the horse was still tied beneath the scrawny trees where it had been left. *Where did he go?* There was a pile of scrap wood, and she wondered if it was for a fire. Hearing footsteps, she turned to duck back under the boulder, only to see him walking toward her with a dead rabbit in his hands. Seeing her awake, he gestured with the rabbit. "Hungry?" he asked. She nodded in response, and he knew then that, as he suspected, she could understand at least some of what he said.

"What is your name?" he asked. Ma-Wi-Taa kept silent. He went about his business of skinning the rabbit, cutting off the meat, and cooking it. When dusk quickly came, he stood and picked up two packs that had been tied to his horse, tossed them down on the ground, and lay down as if to go to sleep. She followed suit, determining she would slip away after he was asleep. Little did she know that, in her exhaustion, she would sleep before him, and that he would lay watching her well into the night.

Louisa

25

Louisa pulled the sleeves of her oversized sweatshirt over her hands as she hiked around the lake trail with her loyal canine walking companion, Abbey. It was a breezy September morning and she was glad she wore leggings instead of shorts. Though the leaves on the trees were still green, she felt the season changing.

Fall was her favorite time of year. It had been as long as she could remember, which is what made getting married to Alan in October even more perfect. Theirs was a short engagement and the wedding was a simple, evening ceremony. The large windows that lined both sides of the church held cream colored candles of varying shapes and sizes on their sills, and the sanctuary glowed from the light they emanated. The reading was from Kahlil Gibran's *The Prophet,* "…but let there be spaces in your togetherness, and let the winds of the heavens dance between you," she recalled.

She was so confident and secure in her decision to marry Alan—not an ounce of doubt did she feel. For two years they had dated and there had always been "spaces in their togetherness," each standing independent yet somehow together. Their friendship was solid, he accepted her for who she was, and they got along so well. She was twenty nine at the time and from her experience, everything about she and Alan was stable. No, she hadn't resolved her feelings for Matthew, but she put them aside as the love of her youth. What else could a person do? It seemed like Matthew had done the same and they were still friends, which was why she didn't hesitate to invite him to the wedding.

She tried to remember if when she said the vow "from this day forward," she on some level suspected she and Alan might part before death, but she couldn't recall. All she could remember was that at that time, she knew she was supposed to be with him. But eight years into it, she no longer knew with the same level of certainty.

The summer had been one of internal change for Louisa and she suspected that in some ways there was no going back. It wasn't just Alan's ever-increasing "traditional marriage" attitude that was the problem, or the fact that it seemed like she and the kids were living a separate life than he. Sure, those things were bothering her, but it was more than that. It was Ojo— maybe not Ojo in and of itself, but the *experience.* She somehow wasn't the same person she was before.

Louisa looked at her watch as she approached the dock. Seven fifteen. There was time to sit and look out over the water for a few minutes. She called Abbey and walked down the ramp to the dock, which Abbey immediately bypassed to wade into the water. Louisa sat down and quickly lost herself in the ripples on the lake's surface. Now what she was thinking about? Ojo? Yes— her marriage and Ojo.

Her Ojo experience was bringing parts of her back to life. She was changing, it was that simple. Not overtly, but in subtle ways. While her circumstances were definitely different than Adelina's, she recognized the power she gave away in relationships and that over the years, she had been giving it away to maintain her marriage too. Slowly but surely, she felt her perspective on her position in her marriage changing and a new sense of empowerment on the horizon.

The revelations that accompanied New Mexico were like a new hobby. She had enrolled herself and Malory in an Anthropology course in early October that went to the sites of Posi and Hupobi, so she would be back in New Mexico in just a few weeks. They would be leaving right after Isaac's birthday, another occasion to make fall her favorite time of year.

She looked up from the water. Did she hear something? She listened intently. "Mommy!" yelled two faint voices as the wind rustled the trees between the dock and her house.

"Time to bust a move Abbey," she called as she jumped up and ran back to the trail. "The kiddos are up!" Abbey followed her to the trail, soaking wet. Louisa scratched the dry hair on top of Abbey's head and the two briskly made their way home.

* * * *

Malory sat on the kitchen floor, leaning against the wall next to the trash can. She had intended on taking it outside, but instead she slumped down to the floor and started crying. The counters were cluttered with dishes that needed to be washed and her dining room table was stacked with mail, her daughter's schoolwork, and laundry that needed to be folded. Did everyone's dining room table get into that state or was it just hers? Tears steamed down her cheeks. For some reason, she was drowning and there was no one there to save her.

But what was she drowning in? *A stagnant cesspool of stagnation.* As the words popped into her head, she sobbed even harder. She reached up to the butcher's block for the roll of paper towels, pulled one off, and blew her very congested nose.

Her silent, self critical dialog continued. She had all day, at least while her daughter was at school, to get stuff done. But she couldn't. She used the sleeve of her sweatshirt to wipe her eyes when her focus fell to the shelf beneath the counter. There she saw her notebook from last year, the corners of papers still sticking out from where they had been haphazardly shoved in. Wind energy. It was moving into western Oklahoma where her family owned farm land. Alternative energy was a cause she could get behind, so for six months she researched, met with a few experts, and tried to start an association of land owners focused on protecting their rights. And then, like she often seemed to do, she set it aside. That time it was because Scott was starting his own business, but come on, even she knew she had issues of follow through.

She thought about calling Louisa but decided not to. It wasn't that Louisa hadn't seen her rendered a pile of rubble before, because she had. Maybe it was just hard to let others see her weaknesses. She rolled her eyes and shook her head with the recognition of yet again another one of her issues. Sometimes life was just too much to think about. She needed relief, a fresh perspective, and she would be getting it in a few days. She and Louisa were going to New Mexico. Thank God for their friendship. Louisa had enrolled them in a day long anthropology class and Malory was looking forward to it. Indigenous people of North America were an interest of hers, and leave it to Louisa to sign them up for a "quick class," as Louisa put it, during their vacation. There was a woman on a mission for you, but hell, Louisa had always been that way; she knew her calling and went straight to it.

Malory smiled to herself and blew her nose into the wadded up paper towel she had been holding. She reached up for the phone to call Louisa and started to dial but quickly hung up instead. Louisa was working and they'd have nine hours in the car to deconstruct her meltdown. With a sigh, she pulled the trash bag out of the can and headed for the back door.

26

They drove in silence after passing through Santa Fe. Eight hours in the car had given the two ample opportunity to catch up on the last few weeks which had not allowed for their usual daily narrative with one another. Louisa looked over and saw Malory with her eyes closed in the reclined passenger seat.

When Malory told her about her breakdown on the kitchen floor, Louisa calmly placed her hand on Malory's arm and asked her "Who do you want to be when you grow up?" The question was simple on the surface, but far more complicated in reality. It isn't just what one might want to do professionally, but what one stands for and where one's energies could be directed. Malory said she didn't know, as Louisa already suspected, which was the point of asking. Malory was one of the most intelligent and vibrant women Louisa knew. If that was to be focused, Malory would be unstoppable, or so it seemed to Louisa.

She had already passed Española and was keeping her eye out for the small highway that would lead them toward Ojo. As she drove further north, the western sun lit up the peaks in the far distance and she thought to herself that they must be at Taos. She passed a visitor center with a statue of a Spaniard on a horse in the parking lot. None of this looked familiar. Had she missed the turn? Next she came upon a sign for Black Mesa Winery and she knew that, in her usual fashion, she had gotten lost. She wouldn't wake Malory—it would only give her more ammunition when she rhetorically asked Louisa how she made it anywhere.

When she saw the chance, she made a u-turn and started back toward Española. Within a few minutes she saw a sign for Ojo Caliente—not the usual route but certainly it would suffice. Louisa turned onto a winding road that led her along the edge of the San Juan Pueblo. The setting sun cast a golden light on the expansive mesa on her right and she wondered if it was Black Mesa as the winery indicated. When she enrolled for the Anthropology class, she had noticed a class that went to a Black Mesa that was overseen by the San Ildefonso Pueblo. She now wondered what the significance of that spot might be.

As the road wound its way along the perimeter of the mesa, Louisa felt the familiar shift in her psyche, unsure if it was accompanied by anticipation or plain fear. She glanced up and saw a raven sitting on the post of a power line. And another. And another. The last one seemed to lock eyes with her, as if it was trying to tell her something. Her throat constricted and as she started to reach for the inhaler in her bag, she broke into a cold sweat. A flash ran before her mind's eye. *I am running.* As panic shot adrenaline through her veins, she made her way around a large curve. *I'm under water.* She pulled the car over onto the narrow shoulder. *As I thrash to get away, I can see the white of his sleeve as he pushes me under the current.*

"What's going on?" asked Malory, sitting up in her seat.

Louisa stared out the windshield with her hands over her mouth. In the distance she saw a car on a road perpendicular to the one they were on, but the intersection was around a boulder and blocked from her view. She looked to the left and saw a line of trees, beyond which she saw water.

"None of this looks familiar," said Malory. "Did you take a wrong turn again?"

Louisa nodded.

"Are you okay?"

"I think so," said Louisa. "I need to get out." She opened her door and crossed the street, followed by Malory. Her white, long sleeve shirt was damp from sweat, as were her black yoga pants, and the cool October air gave her a chill. They climbed through a barbed wire fence and went to the water's edge.

"Do you realize where we are?" asked Malory. "That's the road we usually take to Ojo. See the bridge? Why are we over here?"

"I missed the highway and was headed for Taos. On my way back toward Española I saw a sign for Ojo, so I turned. As I got closer to this spot I couldn't breathe and broke out in a sweat. It's like I was in her body—the woman who drowned. It was the drowning dream, but I was awake."

"This is where you have anxiety and asthma attacks each time we've come here, but it was from the other direction," said Malory. "Any ideas?"

"This is where she drowned," said Louisa.

Malory looked at her with raised eyebrows. Louisa reached over and took Malory's hand. "I don't think— I know."

The two stood in silence for a minute, and when Louisa nodded, Malory turned and used her foot to push down the bottom wire while holding the middle one so Louisa could step through. When she was on the other side, Louisa did the same for Malory. As they walked back to the car, Louisa remembered the three ravens that almost seemed to be speaking to her. She opened the door and climbed back into the driver's seat. "Malory?"

"Yeah?"

"Right before I broke into a sweat, there were three ravens—one right after the other. Do you have your Medicine Cards?"

"I do," Malory said, reaching into the backseat for her bag. "That's weird. Are you sure they weren't crows?"

"Positive," said Louisa, looking over her shoulder and pulling the car back onto the road.

Malory reached into her backpack and pulled out a small blue book. She flipped through the worn pages and read to Louisa. "Raven: Magic. Raven magic is a powerful medicine that can give you the courage to enter the darkness of the void. The void is called the Great Mystery. Raven is the messenger. If Raven appears…you are about to experience a change in consciousness...It would portend a signal brought by Raven that says 'you have earned the right to see and experience a little more of life's magic.'"

"It says that?"

"Yep. I don't know that it could get more prophetic than that."

"But I'm confused," said Louisa. "This spot is a long way from Hupobi. If the woman lived at Hupobi, why was she all the way over here?"

"Give it time, Louisa. It will all unfold. Doesn't it always?"

Louisa looked at Malory and shrugged. "I feel a little sick just thinking about it."

"I bet. Is it time for a little Gordon Lightfoot?" Malory asked and pulled out a CD case.

"Gordon Lightfoot sounds great. I think it's become the official Ojo CD."

Malory pulled the CD out of the case and slipped it into the player. "I'm opening the sunroof babe," she said and then cranked up the heat.

"Look Malory," Louisa said pointing to the landscape. "I absolutely love it here. Love it. I don't think I can get enough of this place."

"As evidenced by the many lifetimes you've lived here."

The two laughed and sang Gordon songs the rest of the way to the springs. When they pulled into the parking lot the sun was setting. The cottonwood trees in their autumn glory of vibrant gold were unlike anything Louisa had seen, and as she looked up at the cliffs, she felt like she had come home.

* * * *

"So the rest of the class is coming from Santa Fe?" asked Malory the following morning as the two sat waiting on a big rock on the edge of the parking lot at the springs.

"Yes, but the archaeologist is coming from Taos, so he is going to meet us here."

"How do you know this?"

"I called him," Louisa said as she pulled her hair back and tucked it into a baseball cap.

"Sounds like you've got it covered. I'll follow your lead."

It was a cool, fall day and the sky was grey. "I'm glad I have my Gortex," Louisa said, watching a man in the distance giving some workers instructions. "Do you think he's in charge here?"

"I don't know," said Malory. "Maybe. Why?"

"The old house by the barn— I need to try and save it from its certain demise." Louisa jumped up and ran over to him calling, "Excuse me? Are you in charge?"

Malory watched Louisa approach him with a smile. From a distance, she could see Louisa speaking with animated gestures, pointing toward the barn and making a large sweeping motion with her arm, perhaps indicating the magnitude of the house's importance. The man—he was kind of cute— pulled his sunglasses down on his nose and stared at Louisa over them. He appeared to be listening intently to what she had to say, but the look on her face was one of stammering. Malory would have loved to have been a fly on the wall to hear that conversation. When Louisa walked back to where she sat on the rock, Malory smiled and asked "How'd that go?"

"I must sound like a crazy woman," she said, making Malory laugh.

"Are you two by any chance waiting to go on up to Posi?" asked a white headed man as he approached them. It was the archaeologist Louisa had spoken to on the phone and he sat down and waited with them for the rest of the group. He pointed out some landmarks in the area, including Black Mesa.

"What's the significance of Black Mesa?" asked Louisa.

"That was where the Tewa fled during the Spanish re-conquest. It was the sight of the final battle with the Pueblo people," he explained. Malory shot a look at Louisa.

"Looks like the group just pulled up. You guys ready?" he asked.

Louisa stood and as the group started toward the trail, she turned and stared at Black Mesa. Pieces quickly came together in her mind; the white puffy sleeve of the person who held the woman under the water. She knew it wasn't someone indigenous to the area. Could it have been a Spaniard? She took a deep breath and followed the group to the trailhead.

They climbed the steep trail that started at the base of the springs to where Louisa had stopped to rest just ten months before. Another ten minutes and they were at Posi, a frequently visited site with trail markings. The archaeologist showed them the highlights, and explained the majority of their time would be spent at Hupobi, which is where they quickly headed.

Hupobi. There it was, right where they had hiked ten months earlier when Louisa was mysteriously pulled in that direction. And of course they didn't notice it on the hill opposite the Rio Ojo; it isn't until you've seen a melted down pueblo that you can identify the barren mountain tops as more than just barren.

And they are anything but barren. As the group walked across what was once the top of an ancient structure that housed up to a thousand people, Louisa began to feel the resonance of life. Pottery shards, dating back more than seven hundred years, were beneath her feet in the sandy earth. She was acutely aware of the connectedness she felt to…what? The place? The people? The land? She didn't know; maybe all of the above. As they hiked farther up, they came to the raised beds used for agriculture. Malory glanced over at her with a wink as if to say, "Here they are Louisa. The levels you dreamed about countless times. They are real. Trust yourself."

Louisa realized she should have done more research in advance; learned what she could about the culture, their Anasazi ancestors, and the history of the land and its people. Of course, that would come in time. She took in what she could in the moment, knowing that visiting the sites opened up new doors of interest and topics to learn about.

Her last night in the springs was quiet and meditative. Aside from her visions by the river, she was calm and centered. While she by no means had all the pieces to the puzzle, her picture of Adelina was somewhat complete and she let the parallels settle into her conscious life. They were obvious, and she gently acknowledged she had some internal work to do. The way her life was unfolding left her filled with awe and she wondered what the strength of that awe would be after another thirty five years of living.

Do we come into this world with agreements that the opportunities to face different challenges will come up at certain points in life? Even though it was almost the end of the year, a friend had printed off an

astrological forecast for Louisa. As she read the last paragraph, she felt it resonate.

"Imagine your life has been divided in half by a screen and all the important changes you feel are developing on the other side... The screen is about to lift, revealing some daring goals you may have forgotten about. If you pursue these goals, the outcome is uncertain, a measure of conviction will be necessary, and you're unlikely to recognize your life when you look back. Thank God for miracles."

Ma-Wi- Taa

27

They sat in an abandoned cliff dwelling dug into the side of the sandstone mountain. A summer storm hovering over the sacred mountains blew over, taking them by surprise. He cradled her face with his hands, and with his thumbs, traced the outline beneath her eyes to wipe away the drops that had landed there. Leaning toward him, she kissed his lips. "I will call you Na-ka-woh-ma," she said.

"Which means?"

"Over and over again like the sunrise; each day you move deeper into my soul."

A full moon had passed since the day she was captured and that first night they had spent together felt far away. She missed her opportunity to sneak away when she fell asleep in the shelter of the bluff, and the next day when she placed her hand on her chest and said "Ma-Wi-Taa," she knew that she made a choice; for some reason she wasn't ready to leave him. She rationalized reasons, such as he would be a source of information for her in the future. When exactly she fell in love with him she wasn't sure. But she knew it was happening by how she felt when she rode behind him, her arms around his waist, and the warmth of his body next to hers when they slept.

She quickly learned she could leave if she chose, and their first day together when he cut the ropes around her wrists, she was free. She came to understand that after he witnessed the executions nine months earlier in Santa Fe, he began to sense he was not of the right mind for the task of conquering the Pueblo people because he fundamentally disagreed. The time he spent with Ma-Wi-Taa made his feelings even stronger.

They moved from place to place when it was safe, perhaps coming across an abandoned farm plot with squash or corn plants that had by nature reseeded themselves the year before. Always watchful for the small contingencies of Spanish soldiers that occasionally passed through the area, as well as those such as herself that chose to leave safety, Ma-Wi-Taa learned that her people were still taking refuge high on the mesa. She occasionally thought about her life there and wondered about her family, but found she felt alive and at peace where she was.

She showed him her homeland and all its beauty. They stayed for a time in the abandoned village where she often went to listen to the ancestors, and traveled a few days north to another abandoned village, below which were the sacred hot waters. Neither knew what their futures held, or what the repercussions of their choices might be. Each day existed separate from the world and the opposing cultures they represented. Together they would stay and another three moons would pass.

* * * *

Louisa

Journal Entry

February 5, 2004

Since my trip in October, I have delved into my studies of New Mexico. My personal library now contains books on the Tewa, the Anasazi, the Pueblo Revolt, and several others. After learning the significance of Black Mesa and my feelings about the drowning location, I read that the Tewa did in fact retreat to Black Mesa during the re-conquest. The Pueblo Revolt was in 1680, meaning the re-conquest would have been in 1692. I still have questions about Hupobi and where that location, inhabited between 1100 and 1300, fits, but for the time being I will do all I can do: wait and see what else is revealed to me.

As I try and assimilate what has been shown to me, I want to understand not only the experiences of Adelina and Ma-Wi-Taa, but the circumstances of their lives. Yet I know that it is not only those cultural and situational factors which in turn helped define their choices and outcomes, but also their perceptions of their experiences.

On a different note, I saw Malory today. She told me she was leaving her marriage. She met someone and knew she was in love. I saw the sparkle in her eye and quite frankly haven't seen her that happy in many years. But the timing of this news has struck me personally. My relationship with Alan is changing, becoming less intertwined. We have spoken of what our future together might look like and that we as a married couple don't work. I think he and I have reached a quiet acceptance. I'm afraid—of losing his friendship, of hurting the kids. But most of all I'm worried that I will end up alone. Alone like Adelina.

Behind my conversation with Malory, I found I was having a dialog within myself wondering what it is that makes us leave one relationship for another. Is it the coming back to life that comes with falling in love, or is it our undying hope that whoever we hold in the position of significant other will in some way be better than the person who held that position before? And as these thoughts passed through my mind, I wondered what my situation would be. If I leave my marriage, will it be with the intention of finding someone else or will I first face my self and stand alone?

I have begun to classify my responses in life. I tell myself "this is an Adelina response," when I am feeling cast aside, fearful or alone. When I am in touch with the independent, forging ahead in life part of myself, I feel like Ma-Wi-Taa.

When it comes to the notion of my marriage ending, I am very much "Adelina." She was alone, and while in ways she was strong, her strength was one of hardened self protection. I don't want to become that, and I pray every night before I go to sleep for Spirit to hold me and guide me where I need to be.

Adelina

28

There was laughing outside the doorway to the small room where Adelina worked, where the mostly anglo patrons of the springs gathered around the pools. Sweat beaded along the hairline of her forehead and the sleeves of her blouse were pushed up over her elbows. Rumor was there were uniforms coming, a sign that times were changing, but on this hot summer day her bloomers stuck to her skin beneath her long skirt.

She rubbed the linens on the washboard in rhythmic fashion, her mind far from the drudgery that defined her days. As she turned the piece she was scrubbing over, she scraped her knuckle and blood ran into the water. She grabbed her finger and squeezed it to stop the sting. With a deep sigh, she walked over and looked out the doorway.

While the world had rapidly changed around her, Adelina's life was the same. Her days were filled with hard work, and in the evenings, she went to sleep alone, in preparation to do it all again the next day.

Her contact with Antonio was sparse while he worked to secure his seat as a Territorial representative, which he lost in 1904. Adelina had been hopeful that he would return to Ojo Caliente for good. But in spite of that, she had seen him very little over the past year and was forced to accept whatever it was he was willing to give.

She walked back to her washboard and continued with her work, knowing she could not leave that night until the pile next to her was gone. She heard voices approaching from outside.

"Who's the father?" asked the young woman.

"Señor Silva," said another.

"The son?"

"No, Sofia is the new mistress. Señor Silva is the father of the baby."

The two young women walked in the door, saw Adelina and quickly silenced themselves as they went into the back room. Her heart pounded so loudly she could hear the rush of blood in her ears and she silently repeated the words she had just heard.

Her head was spinning and her emotion so strong she felt nauseas. She walked as fast as she could toward the dirt road that ran along the river. Blurred by her tears, she was lost in the betrayal. As she made the curve to their meeting place, her safe haven, she let herself fall to her knees in the dirt. No one was there to see her pain or hear her sobs. She was alone, as she essentially had been all her life. She only fooled herself that she wasn't.

Three weeks of isolation crept by in which Adelina was unable to eat, sleep or work. Funny that no one had even checked on her. From deep in the hole in which she found herself, she wondered where her life had gone and how it could have been different. Was her love for Antonio so strong she could see nothing else? Or was she simply unable to break free? Of course the answers to those questions didn't matter anymore, and for the first time, she knew she could never love him again—not like she had before.

She knelt by the river, scrubbing her clothes. As the water rushed over the rocks, she stopped what she was doing and stared. She felt herself merge with the river and lose herself in its flow, longing to be swept away from herself. Her trance was broken when she heard the familiar sound of someone on horseback approaching.

Leaving her work where it was, she made her way through the small trees and brush that lined the river and saw Antonio step onto the porch and knock on the door. She felt dead inside, unable to speak. Antonio turned and saw her.

"I haven't seen you in church. Your account shows you haven't been into the Mercantile in weeks."

"How could you do this to me?" she said numbly.

"Do what?"

"I have loved you for almost twenty years. You made certain no one would have me, and then you leave me alone. I know about Sofia."

"I owe you no explanations."

"Of course not. You take what you want from others with no consideration for what you leave in your wake."

"I think you have forgotten your place," he said, stepping toward her with a raised hand.

"You can hit me, Antonio. I have survived it before. You can't hurt me any more than you already have. You controlled my life. You made certain no one else would ever want me, and I have spent my life alone. My daughter is dead, my son doesn't know I am his mother. You have taken everything that matters."

Antonio looked at her worn, gaunt face with contempt. "Why would I want you? You were once beautiful. Now look at you. Your hands are calloused. No man would want them to touch him."

"You are dead to me," she said as she stepped past him. She went inside and closed the door, listening as he rode away. And as the stomping of hooves grew more and more faint, she slid to the ground and found there were more tears to be cried.

Was it what she wanted? She didn't know. But her pain was too deep to recover.

Five years later Adelina would privately grieve the death of the man she never stopped loving. Antonio passed away in 1910.

Louisa

29

Louisa turned on the electric blanket to warm up the sheets, then stacked the pillows against the headboard to prop herself up. It was a cold night in late February and Isaac and Caleb lay next to her where they had fallen asleep, waiting for her to get home. She reached over and covered them up with the blanket.

"How was dinner?" asked Alan as he walked in and stroked Isaac's hair.

"It was good. Thanks for watching the boys," said Louisa slipping her feet under the covers.

"How's Paco?" he asked.

"Paco?"

"You know, the guy Matthew was."

"You mean Antonio."

"Yeah. I can't keep it all straight."

Louisa smiled and nodded. "Matthew seems to be doing well. It was good to see him. I appreciate you being okay with me meeting him."

Alan leaned across the bed and stroked both the boys' heads, then did the same to Louisa. "You two have unfinished business," he said, and walked back into the living room.

Louisa had met Matthew for dinner after her meetings in Oklahoma City, which lay half way between the towns where they lived. They had only seen each other twice since she got married, not because they couldn't so much as their lives had grown so very different. She took the career, wife, and mother path. Matthew never married, owned a bar in a college town and lived very much like a man in his early twenties.

The decision to meet was what one could call an "apparently irrelevant decision" that probably wasn't irrelevant at all, and on some level Louisa knew it. For the past year she and Matthew had kept in touch and at the same time Alan had been withdrawing from their marriage. Alan had even commented several times that she should have an affair, leading her to question if he wanted the appearance of marriage rather than the relationship itself. From her perspective, an affair was the beginning of the end. But if a husband would rather his wife get her needs for companionship met elsewhere, was it already in some form the end? Regardless, she met Matthew for dinner.

As Louisa and Matthew sat together that night, she felt the familiar comfort of his friendship. It would probably always be that way, regardless of their contact with one another. It had been great to see him, wonderful in fact, and when she hugged him goodbye she felt that familiar twinge of not wanting to let go. Yet she was keenly aware of the dynamic that had existed between them and how she allowed it to play over and over again like a worn out recording. Much of what she had struggled with about herself was magnified when she thought about their past—not believing she deserved to be treated better. When it came down to it, how different was she than Adelina? She wasn't— when it had come to Matthew, in many ways she was Adelina in different clothes.

She settled into the pillows with her hand on Caleb's back, her mind too active to sleep. As an adult, would Matthew ever comprehend the subtle magnitude of his own actions? Would he ever understand that being young doesn't cause the footprints you leave behind to be erased? The fact that she cared made her loathe herself even more, and in that moment, she decided it was time to work through it and move on.

Now the question of *how* was a different matter altogether, far more complicated than the declaration itself. It was also a matter of more than just Matthew. She pulled the Seth book out of the drawer in seek of an answer. She flipped through the chapter titled "Reincarnational Dramas."

"Throughout your reincarnational existences, you expand your consciousness, your ideas, perceptions and your values. You break away from self adopted restrictions and grow spiritually as you learn to step aside from limiting concepts and dogma.

From within your point of reference it is often difficult for you to perceive all events work toward creativity, or to trust the spontaneity of your own natures...Someone very well known once said 'Turn the other cheek...' You should turn the other cheek because you realize that basically the attacker only attacks himself.

Now all of this can be applied to your relationships in your reincarnational existences, and of course it is highly pertinent to your daily experience. If you hate another person, that hate may bind through as many lives as you allow the hate to consume you. You draw to yourself in this existence and in all others those qualities upon which you concentrate your attention. If you vividly concern yourself with the injustices you feel have been done to you, then you attract more such experiences...[4]

If you examine your life now, carefully, the challenges you have set for yourself will be apparent. This is not easy to do, but it is within the grasp of each individual. Knowing your reincarnational background, but not knowing the nature of your present self, is useless. You cannot justify or rationalize present circumstances by saying 'This is because of something I did in a past life' for within yourself NOW is the ability to change negative influences. You may have brought negative influences into your life for a given reason, but the reason always has to do with understanding, and understanding removes influences."[5]

---

[4] (Roberts, pp. 170-171)

[5] (Roberts, p. 181)

Louisa re-read the last paragraph carefully. *"If you vividly concern yourself with the injustices you feel have been done to you, then you attract more such experiences."* In that moment, she felt an understanding lock into place. *"Knowing your reincarnational background, but not knowing the nature of your present self, is useless."*

She turned back in the book to a section she had read before and found the sentences underlined. *"You have the knowledge of your entire multidimensional personality at your fingertips…<u>When</u> you realize that you do, this knowledge allows you to solve problems or meet the challenges you have set, more quickly, in your terms…"*

She had the knowledge, so she needed to use it. Perhaps that was a part of why she and Matthew had come back into each other's lives, to reach a level of reconciliation. A reconciliation that would be as much within themselves individually as it would be about each other. And perhaps, in the spirit of simultaneous lives having the ability to impact one another, that reconciliation within her could in turn help Adelina.

As she lay down to go to sleep, she found herself wondering if she was up to whatever challenge she was undertaking, and as she closed her eyes, she asked Spirit to show her more.

* * * *

She is in another body, sitting by a river and holding a baby that she knows to be about six weeks old. The infant rests in her lap and those with authority tell her the baby's life must be terminated. The people, while unfamiliar in looks, were people of power she knew through her profession. Understanding what she must do, she lifts the baby and places it under the river's surface.

Louisa jolted up in her bed. Knowing she was going to be ill, she rushed to the bathroom. The tile floor was painful on her knees as she wretched, but it paled in comparison to the horrifying image of the drowning infant now imprinted in her memory.

Thunder Cloud
30

Thunder Cloud stood on the second level of the pueblo, facing southeast. With nine hundred ground room floors and three hundred rooms on the second level, he felt small as he looked across the three plazas within his view. His hair was pulled tightly back and wrapped into a ball on the back of his head and he stood with his arms folded over his chest. Wearing deer skin pants, a thick woven shirt, and a small bone holding his wrapped hair in place, he squinted as he surveyed his surroundings. The long, dark mesa to the south spread across his view and he surveyed the sacred mountain peaks that rose in both directions. Below him in the plaza, children scurried about playing, and a group of young women, including his wife, sat talking and grinding dried corn. Behind him there were farm plots that terraced the rocky mountainside, and scattered groups of people skillfully navigated the terrain, bringing squash and ears of corn toward the pueblo to be hung and dried. Rains had come that year and his people were in good favor with the spirits.

The tribe had lived in this place called Hupobi for many sun cycles. Their ancestors had come from the north. They were driven out of their homes around the cliffs on the great Mesa. Traveling south, they re-inhabited the buildings of the Old Ones. Over the past two hundred years, the story of the fall of the Old Ones had become unclear. Hostile raiders? Severe drought? Cultural breakdown? Religious wars? Word of the Katsina's had spread across the lands, and the believers professed that these spirits of the ancestors would help them please the Gods, thus bringing rain. Perhaps the new religion had been a response to the many troubled times. Regardless, the inhabitants of that great culture dispersed, and those that traveled south set up villages along the river. Their stories and traditions would take different directions as the years would pass, and in essence, each tribe would become its own people.

The people at Hupobi believed their original ancestors came from beneath a sandy lake far to the north, where men, the supernatural, and animals lived together and death was unknown. Of these Supernatural beings were the two first mothers of their people; Blue Corn Mother for the Summer and White Corn Mother for the Winter. One of the mothers asked a man to seek out a way that their people might leave the lake. He went in the four directions and found nothing but mist and haze. He was then instructed to go above the lake, and the land there was ready. After the animals there accepted him, they gave him a bow and arrow, and he became Hunt Chief. He was the first Made person and went back to the lake, where he gave ears of white corn to two men who would also become Made people; one who would guide the people during the summer, and one during the winter. The people were then divided into two groups; the summer people traveled down one side of the river and the winter people down the other, each making stops and building villages along the way. The summer and winter people then united here, at a village near the sacred hot springs.

These stories he did not question. Nor did he question the authority within the pueblo. These were the rules to live by and defined each person's duty.

He had known Flower Morning since he was a child, at a time when they played together in the plaza like the children he was watching today. Things were good then, weren't they? Warfare was less common. It seemed like the differentiation between those with power and those without was less noticeable then. Was ignorance bliss?

Flower Morning's father was the Summer Chief and was revered by the tribe for his even handedness and gentle authority. He achieved this status by marriage, as his wife was the first born daughter of the highest ranking woman in the pueblo, and it was the women who controlled both status and property within the tribe. This line of power led to the arranged marriage between Thunder Cloud and Flower Morning; the Summer Chief was in essence selecting his successor by arranging for the marriage of his oldest daughter who would one day be the Head Mother of the village. Such decisions were essential inasmuch that the Chiefs made warfare decisions, and times had long been turbulent with raiding tribes from the North and unpredictable rains.

For eight years he had been in marriage with Flower Morning, from which early on came a son. He loved his wife, as best he knew how, but emotion wasn't something he gave much consideration. He accepted the union as the way it was and he had duties to fulfill. Duty and responsibility were his way of viewing his life, and he did this with pride and commitment. He cared for his family as he should and he would teach his son what he needed to know to become a man within the tribe; how to hunt, fish, and go into battle.

Flower Morning respected these qualities in her husband, yet at the same time found them dull and cold. To her he seemed lifeless in ways; unable to reach out and touch the wind. She too, cared for her family as she should, and her son was the center of her world, but she had often found her spirit drifting elsewhere, wanting to fill herself with something alive. Thunder Cloud had always known this about her and accepted it as he did the rest of his life; it was what it was.

They were Made people; their role was to make up the political organization and leadership within the tribe. The life of a made person was quite different than the Weed People, or commoners. There were different expectations. Choices had different implications. These he contemplated as he looked out over the pueblo, waiting for the council to emerge from the kiva.

*   *   *   *

Flower Morning sat against the wall of the pueblo in the plaza with two other women. Her long black hair hung loose and strands blew around her face. She wore a long, straight dress and a woven blanket draped across her shoulders. The two other mothers had their babies in cradle boards, propped against the wall as they used their *metates* to grind the corn into a coarse meal. Flower Morning heard bits and pieces of the conversation. She looked down at her newborn daughter, alive now for less that two moons, and was lost in her own feelings.

There were no words to describe the bond between mother and her child; the intangible, all consuming power that relationship holds. As she nursed, she breathed it in, letting it fill her life soul, but in a quiet desperation. She looked up and saw her husband. He looked severe with his hair tightly pulled back and his harsh expression.

She tuned into the conversation next to her and heard the questioning of the others.

"The elders went into the kiva just after dawn? Has something happened? I heard the traders that came through yesterday speaking of raids not far from here. Perhaps there is concern."

"I hope not," said the other woman. "This is the first decent season of rains. Our food storage is low. I fear our harvest will be taken by the wandering tribes, that we are not safe, and that the hard times my Grandmother spoke of are coming again."

Flower Morning turned away. She knew the elders were not discussing the raids, or the harvest, or the coming of hard times. They were discussing her, her decisions, and the life of her baby.

She had met Soaring Hawk as she traveled the road between their pueblo and the one to the south. She had met with the Head Mother there on behalf of her mother, whose health had been declining. He was a trader she had seen in her village. He was young, strong, and went where the wind took him. As they spoke the first time, she felt the freedom he possessed and longed to make it her own. Over the months, he passed through their village more often and a relationship developed, though superficial at first. Over time it grew deeper, and she found herself creating reasons to travel between the neighboring villages to have the opportunity to be alone with him.

When she went for three moons without her cycle, she knew she was with a child. She could have taken the tea and terminated the pregnancy, but chose not to. She wanted it, and wanted what it represented to her; a freedom of sorts.

Flower Morning held her husband in high regard in many ways: his leadership, responsibility, his steadfast manner in making decisions. For these reasons she didn't speak the truth until the day he asked for it. He had suspected, hadn't he? That day he returned from a hunt and saw her standing in the plaza laughing and talking with the young trader from the south? He saw the way she brightened in his presence, and the way she had reason to leave the village for periods of time when he was passing through. But Thunder had chosen to let those things pass, and to proceed with the predictable life he chose to live.

When she told him the truth, she saw the hurt in his eyes, but he rarely spoke of his feelings. He simply reminded her of her duties to her people, that it would weaken her future position if the truth was to be discovered, and instructed her to tell the father he was no longer welcome in their village. This would be their secret, which would be best for all concerned. And so it would be for the remainder of the pregnancy. She would never see Soaring Hawk again, and he would never know of their child. The baby was born, Flower Morning's first daughter.

Shortly after the birth, there were preparations for the naming ceremony, and Thunder Cloud sat with Sun Breath, the Priest and vision keeper of the tribe.

"Thunder Cloud, I had a disturbing vision last night," said Sun Breath.

"Yes?"

"The Spirits of the Ancient Ones came to me. They flew over the sacred mountains to the east, and one spoke to me of trouble for our people. Foreign ones were coming from an opening in the ground in the South, and our ways would be lost. This message, it must be carried forward. Our people will lose their ways without a strong leader."

He nodded in silence as the elder spoke; the same wise man who helped reach the Spirits and brought rain, who prepared their dead for passing, and brought wisdom from the ancestors. He had spoken to Thunder of the future. The words scared him. Would he as Chief be the leader that would have to save their people? Would it be the next generation, or the next?

That night he tossed and turned, unable to rest. He feared the actions of he and Flower Morning would play a part of what might lead to the end of their people and their way of life as they knew it. Duty, obligation, and integrity to the tribe—these were the characteristics that defined him. The next morning he told his wife of Sun Breath's vision and of his fears.

"This child," he said gesturing toward the baby, "will become Head Mother of our people. Yet she was born of adultery, and the Spirits know of this truth."

"You don't know that the vision will come to life. It may be many sun cycles from now, when we have all gone to the Spirits," Flower Morning pleaded. But she knew she couldn't stop him from doing what he felt was right.

"I will speak with the priest, and he will tell me what we should do."

With those words, he left their home. Flower Morning sat in fearful silence as he walked away, holding her baby.

* * * *

Dogs barked and ran to the entry of the plaza as a small group of men returned from an early morning hunt. They brought with them a small doe and a few rabbits, and the children followed the dogs over to the men. The sounds brought Flower Morning back to the present, where she sat against the wall with the two other women, no longer discussing what was transpiring in the kiva, but silently working again. Movement caught her eye and she saw Thunder Cloud coming down the ladder and walking toward Sun Breath, who had come out of the kiva.

When Thunder Cloud had spoken to the priest about the baby, Sun Breath listened patiently and intently on the story shared with him. Still burdened by his vision, he too saw that the violation of the tribe's norms when Morning Flower bore a child that wasn't her husband's, and that while the tribe as a whole need not be made aware, the issue should be taken to the tribal elders in leadership roles. It would be they who decided what should be done.

Thunder Cloud glanced in the direction of his wife as he walked toward the kiva entrance, and as their eyes met, he saw the deep fear and concern in her eyes. He gestured to her to come with him and she rose and walked in his direction. They climbed down the ladder where they stood before the chief and his wife, the priest, and three other elders. Flower Morning glanced at her parents to see her mother looking down.

Her father spoke. "You have placed us in a very difficult position. We have learned that your husband is not the father of this baby. You have duties to your people. Have you forgotten this? You will lead one day soon, and this child as your daughter will someday lead as well. How will your people trust you if they learn the truth that this child was born out of adultery? How could she ever lead them?"

Sun Breath interjected, "Flower Morning, we fear for the stability of our people in these turbulent times."

"Yes, Thunder Cloud shared your vision with me," she said.

The Chief spoke again. "This is something that must not be made known to the commoners. My daughter, you are not one of them, free to lay with whomever you wish. Your husband is to be Chief; we have chosen him. You cannot simply set his things by the door and send him away when you wish to be done with him as the commoners can."

One of the other Elders spoke up. "We have a responsibility to our people to make sure that we are strong. Without strong leaders that are respected and revered by the people, we will be easy targets for the raiders from the north. We will have chaos in battle. We will become factions like in the days of our great grandparents."

"The Council will decide. You may both go," said the Chief. Thunder Cloud and Flower Morning climbed the ladder and left the kiva.

The bright sun shocked their eyes as they entered the plaza, and they squinted as they started walking. Without looking at him, she asked, "What do you think they will do?"

"I do not know," he said, then paused. "Your betrayal has created many problems, Flower, many problems." Saying nothing else, he walked away.

* * * *

Louisa

Journal Entry

October 3, 2005

I last wrote in February of 2004. Alan moved into a house a few miles away and we are settling into a new way of being. It's been a year of gradual change, taking deep breaths, and getting centered in my self.

In the midst of my life changes, I stopped remembering my dreams. It saddened me to think that my Ojo experience was over, but I can now see that I have been applying my realizations of "self" in the most practical of ways. I have found myself grappling with my deepest insecurities; fears of being abandoned and alone, of not being wanted, and of failing my children. More than ever I am beginning to see how my most intimate relationships mirror those fears and I am trying to embrace those relationships as my teachers. I am beginning to understand that perception is reality, and I don't have to look through the lens of those fears any longer. I seek daily wisdom from Spirit, and hope that it is possible to view the end of a marriage with love. "All events work toward creativity," Seth said, regardless of if we define those events as good or bad.

But lately more dreams are beginning to penetrate my awareness, and while it seems impossible that more could be coming, I once again feel the push of psychic energy that, until this past year, had become an integral part of my life. For now I will wait patiently for more.

31

Was there such a thing as fate? It was something Louisa at times wondered about. In many ways she believed in destiny. But she also believed in free will— that individuals make choices that in turn determine their "fate." She could look at her own life and say that it seemed like destiny that she went to Ojo, for example. Certainly the events of the past few years were more than coincidence. Perhaps there was a truth that lie somewhere in the middle. Maybe, just maybe, we come into this world with the agreement that certain opportunities would arise at certain points in our lives, but we also hold the ability to choose which opportunities we seize.

Such thoughts she pondered on one cool November morning. Louisa showered before the boys woke up and went out to the kitchen to start breakfast. She emptied the dishwasher, put cold packs in the lunchboxes and made a cup of tea. She felt unsettled but couldn't identify why.

Regardless of her awareness of it, fate was at hand. An agreement of sorts had been made, and across town was a woman also preparing her children for school and making breakfast before she too had to leave: for a job interview with a woman named Louisa.

Candace dropped her eight year old son off at school. She pulled out of the drive and watched in the rear view mirror as he ran up the sidewalk to the front doors. As she drove away from him, she found herself getting choked up. What was it about seeing him walk away from her that caused her to have that response? She took a finger and ran it along her lower eyelid to wipe away any moisture that could cause her eyeliner to run, then checked her face in the mirror. She took a deep breath and let it out. Her focus needed to be on the interview she had in fifteen minutes.

She looked down at the sticky note where she had written the directions to the Juvenile Center. She had been a child welfare worker in Montana, so when she saw the ad in the paper for a position with this particular child advocacy organization, her familiarity led her to apply. Those were the good old days—in Montana that is. Not that she was free from trials there, because she had many: marital problems, breast cancer, just to name a few. But there were significant people there who helped her through it, one in particular. His support got her through a partial mastectomy and losing her hair. Montana was where she wanted to be, in her heart, but when she and her husband decided to reconcile, it ultimately meant moving.

Candace walked into the sage green office lit by several small lamps. No one was at the front desk, but a woman with shoulder length hair, blue eyes and a big smile stepped out of the back office to greet her.

"You must be Candace," she said, smiling. "I'm Louisa. Come on back."

Candace followed her into the office and took a seat across from Louisa.

"After our conversation on the phone and looking at your resume again, I really think you'd be a good addition to our staff," said Louisa. "I have some more questions for you. Hopefully they'll help you determine if you think this organization would be a good fit for you."

Candace nodded and answered Louisa's questions. They seemed to be getting at intrinsic motivation, flexibility, adaptability and the like. As she engaged Louisa in this dialog, she felt herself at a distance; like she was hovering, observing rather than the one experiencing it. She pressed her back into the cushion and gripped the arm rests of the chair. Yes, she was still in the chair. She concentrated on Louisa's face to stay present. As she looked into her eyes, she felt something. Tony. She felt Tony—who got her through chemo. Not that this woman interviewing her was Tony, but that she herself was in some way connected to Tony through Louisa. She swallowed hard.

When Louisa asked her if she thought this was a place she would like to work, she didn't hesitate to say yes. Louisa told her she would contact her as soon as a background check was complete and thanked her for coming in. Candace thanked her for the opportunity, walked out of the office and to her car. She felt like she had had too much to drink—not quite in her body. She unrolled the windows and let the cool air blow through the car, bringing her back to normality. Whatever was happening didn't really frighten her, but it was pretty damn strange.

* * * *

Journal Entry

December 8, 2005

My sleep has grown more and more restless and disturbed. Each time I wake I come back with images of water and people I know from work: Directors of other child advocacy programs, a judge, etc. By the tone of these dream fragments I know they are related to New Mexico. I have had the dream about drowning the infant again, and again there were people I know professionally.

It led me to ask the question: how would a whole group of people come back together? I wanted to see what kind of information existed on the subject so I went to the internet. Much to my surprise, there are books written on that very matter, one of which I ordered and am now reading. Mission to Millboro is about a group of people that live somewhere in California who in a previous life lived in a little town in Virginia during the Civil War. Through hypnotherapy, individuals gave graphic descriptions of the town, their names, and so on.

I also referred to the Seth material, which I am coming to hold as my metaphysical bible. I scanned the pages and found an initial reference to group reincarnation.

You have made appointments, each of you, that you have forgotten. They were signed, so to speak, before you came into this existence...

Realize also that towns and villages may also be composed of the past inhabitants of other such towns and villages, transposed with new experiences and backgrounds as the group tries different experiments. Now sometimes, there are also such variations in that the inhabitants of a particular town may be reborn inhabitants of those who lived, say in 1632 in a small Irish village. They may be transposed to a town in Idaho.

...Information concerning these is often given to you in the sleep state, and there is a kind of gestalt type of dream, a root dream, by which those who have known each other in past lives communicate. In such dreams, general mass information is given, that the individuals then use as they desire. Overall plans for development are made, as the group members, say of a town, decide its destiny. Some individuals always choose to be reborn as a part of some group—reborn, in other words, with past contemporaries...[6]

[6](Roberts, p. 176)

I find myself wondering, could this network of passionate individuals in my professional community have been inhabitants of the Pueblo world, transposed with new experiences and backgrounds, trying a different group experiment? The more I learn about the subject of groups incarnating together, the more I begin to see the many layers of those professional relationships. Now, with more questions than ever, I wonder if I will ever find out.

32

The holidays came and went. While she had settled into a new status quo, Louisa felt a sense of frustration, like it was time to branch out of her comfort zone, and her New Year's resolution was "adventure." Adventure can come in many forms and she should have realized that when she made the request of the universe. Maybe she had travel in mind, or a passionate romance. Perhaps she should have been more specific because her adventure was coming, and because of the form it would take, she would view it as anything but positive.

She sat next to the Christmas tree with Isaac and Caleb next to her on the couch, one tucked under each arm. She had done it again—left the tree up well into January. She wondered if this year it was because she was immobilized. Not in a falling apart kind of way, but in a subtle form of depression kind of way. She and Alan had worked out the details of the divorce to submit to the attorney right before the holidays and at times it was a lot to digest. But on this cold Saturday afternoon, a fire gently burned in the fireplace and the boys had roasted marshmallows for s'mores. Their hands and faces were covered with melted chocolate and sticky, melted marshmallow. She felt the deep, inner content of being with them, and in moments like this, she remembered what was really important: happy, healthy children.

The phone rang and Louisa looked at the clock, wondering who it could be. She quickly got up and walked to the study.

"Hello?" she said.

"Hi Louisa. It's Candace."

"Hi! How's your weekend?"

"It was good until this morning when I got a call from a child welfare worker," said Candace.

"What's going on?" asked Louisa.

"There was a staffing on the Walsh case right before Christmas. Child Welfare wanted the judge to dismiss the abuse case, leaving only the mental health case open."

"How old is the child again?" asked Louisa, shutting the glass door to the study and taking a seat in the green overstuffed chair by the front widow.

"He's twelve," said Candace.

"Wait," said Louisa. "Why would they want to close the deprived case? I thought he hadn't seen his parents in months."

"He hadn't seen them— for almost a year," said Candace, "but the court ordered a trial unsupervised visitation, which we spoke up against. Then I got a call early this morning from the social worker. She told me the child was raped last night. The details aren't clear, but he was in his mother's bed. There is a man, not high functioning, that the father gets drugs from in exchange for sex with the mother. I guess he had sex with the child instead. What's worse is that this is the same man who raped him three years ago, leading to court intervention in the first place."

Louisa felt a twinge in the pit of her stomach, then pushed it aside and focused. "So where is he now?"

"I don't know yet," said Candace. "He was taken in for a rape exam and I'm not sure where he will be placed next."

"We need to push for him to go back to where he was placed before, if at all possible. But we also need to work with the District Attorney's office and the child's attorney and push for termination of parental rights."

"I agree," said Candace. "He hasn't been placed with his parents for three years. They show no interest in parenting him."

"Or the need to protect," added Louisa. "Thanks for keeping me informed Candace."

"I'll call you when I know more," said Candace and then said goodbye.

Louisa hung up the phone and went out to the living room, taking her place between Isaac and Caleb, now done with their s'mores. She felt the tears building in her eyes. It's not that the subject matter at work didn't ever bother her—it did. But over the years her skin had gotten thick. She learned to separate herself out from the *reality* and think in terms of responses. It was a coping mechanism and one that had served her well for many years, but it was now failing her. She felt nauseas and hot. A twelve year old boy raped by the same man that raped him three years ago? How could the system fail him like that? She got up and walked to the kitchen, ran a washcloth under the faucet, then placed it on her neck.

Deciding a distraction would be good, she grabbed the sponge and began to aggressively clean the counter tops. She scrubbed all of them and then picked up the unopened mail to wipe beneath it. In the pile was a jury summons. *Great.* She shoved it aside with disrespect; there was no such thing as justice—at least not on this earth. The shortcomings of the judicial system were clearly evident by the phone call from Candace. She stopped scrubbing and looked over at the boys. In that moment she saw a fleeting image of Isaac being assaulted. She shouldn't have let her thoughts go there—but it happened before she had a chance to stop herself. She slid down to the floor with her back against the cabinet, sobbing as quietly as she could.

The front door opened, and Alan walked into the kitchen and threw his keys on the counter. He looked down and saw Louisa on the floor. "Weezie? What's going on?" he asked, kneeling down next to her.

She shook her head, afraid to let him comfort her. He pulled her into his arms and held her while she cried.

"Tell me what's wrong," he said again.

"The kids," she said, speaking in a whisper.

"What's wrong with the kids?" he asked quietly.

"We can't protect them."

Alan had seen Louisa deeply affected by work only once before, years ago before they were married. A child had been beaten to death and his remains put in an empty deep freezer and covered with dirt. It pushed her close to the edge and for a time he thought she would leave social work altogether. That was when she started massage therapy school, which she loved. But the reality was that social work was in her heart and he couldn't imagine her doing anything else, at least not for a while. Rarely did she internalize the cases, which was what he guessed anyone would have to learn to do if they were going to work in that profession.

Apparently her guard was down this time; she had definitely internalized. But there was more to it than work. All mothers worried about being able to protect their children, he got that. But after Isaac was born, Louisa was a crazy woman. Not in the hormonal post-partum, overprotective about details and cleanliness kind of way you often see with new mothers; it was her paranoia that someone was going to take him. For almost a year she kept lights on throughout the entire house at night, and she had dreams that someone took him. Then once, when she was pregnant with Caleb, she was at home ill. Pregnancy was hard on Louisa and she had been hospitalized for severe dehydration the weekend before. She called him at work, hysterical. She said she had a dream that she was another woman with two children, school age, and they were naked and being shoved aggressively by man in a khaki shirt. When she woke up, she had a complete breakdown. She "knew" it was a holocaust scene. She told him she understood why she had hard pregnancies: she didn't feel worthy of her children because she couldn't protect them.

All this Ojo-reincarnation stuff was out of his league. It seemed like a bunch of voo-doo to him, and quite frankly, he didn't think she ever needed to go there again. But when Louisa told him about the dream she had, the one with the baby that was taken from her, and then that the woman in New Mexico had two children taken from her? Well, it made some things make sense. Now she was in a dark hole he could in no way understand, so he did the only thing he knew to do: he called Malory.

Within twenty minutes Malory walked through the front door without knocking. Alan simply pointed in the direction of the bedroom, where she found Louisa curled up on the bed.

Louisa rolled over and saw her. "I had a meltdown."

"I know sweetie, that's why I'm here. Alan already told me about the work stuff that set you off," said Malory, curling up on the bed facing Louisa. "I think there is more to your response than work; it's about you.

"Maybe," Louisa said, sniffing.

"Well, tell me the surface layer of what's bothering you," said Malory.

Louisa wiped the tears from her cheeks. "This damn system I work within—it's so screwed up. For some reason it's catching up with me. And now I have jury duty. I don't think I can do it."

"Jury duty? When is it?"

Louisa shook her head that she didn't know. "The summons is on the kitchen counter."

"Is this going to keep us from going to Ojo next week?"

Louisa shook her head, saying no.

"Wait. I read in the paper about a special jury pool that was just called," said Malory. "Oh my God."

"What?" said Louisa, reaching for a tissue.

"Louisa, it's for that rape- murder case where the girl was drowned. Remember? It happened ten years ago."

Louisa started to sob. "Yes, I remember. She lived a mile from my house. For weeks I choked up as I drove past the apartment complex where she lived, the story was so horrible. Of all things—I can't deal with this right now."

"Do you not see what's happening?" asked Malory, her eyes wide. "It's the next part. It's time —the girl that drowned—-that indigenous life. This is a signpost."

"I don't want to deal with this."

"It's clear you're dealing with some victimization karma," Malory continued, processing her own stream of thought. "Interesting."

"Thanks Dr. Malory," Louisa said with sarcasm.

"Louisa, this is really exciting," said Malory, rubbing Louisa's hand in maternal fashion.

"It doesn't feel exciting. I'm a mess." Louisa grabbed another tissue and blew her nose.

"But you're being thrown a medicine ball."

"Maybe so, but I don't know that it's one that I want to catch."

Malory laughed. "I think you must have already agreed to it or none of this would have happened in the first place."

"All this intangible drama—why can't I just be normal?" asked Louisa, rhetorically.

"It's way past that option, sweetie," said Malory, "way past."

Louisa let out a deep breath and sat up. "I guess it's time for me to go be a mother. One minute we're eating s'mores and the next I'm hiding in here so they won't see me upset."

"They were watching a movie when I came in—oblivious to the fact that their mother was having a breakdown," said Malory with a smile as they both stood up. "Do we need to talk about your fears about protecting your children right now, or can you think about where some of it may be stemming from on your own?"

"I'll work on it," said Louisa, giving Malory a hug. "Thanks."

"Like I always tell you," said Malory. "It'll be my turn soon."

Later that night as she tried to sleep, Louisa's feelings from earlier in the day resurfaced. She found herself thinking about the e-mail from the psychic she received before her first trip to Ojo. She walked to her desk and woke up the computer. Going to Google, she found the website and wrote her question.

> *"I think I am going to be getting some information on an indigenous lifetime in New Mexico. I was also called for jury duty in a pool that is specifically for a rape/murder case, and I'm having an intense emotional response. Is there a relationship between the two?"*

She sent the question off into cyberspace and prayed her stress would go off with it. She went back to the bedroom and crawled into the warm bed. Her angel boys were asleep next to her, and she put her arm across them, thanked God for their presence in her life, and allowed herself to rest.

33

Her whole day was ruined when she got the early morning call from the Child Welfare worker, and Candace had gone to bed early. She was asleep, or she thought she was asleep. She saw a shadow box, so she must have been dreaming. This hadn't happened in several years, but back then she thought it was a side effect of the chemo. But she wasn't going through chemo anymore, and here was the shadow box image again. In the different sections she saw fires burning here and there, people at work, some sitting with their families. She stirred and rolled over onto her side, then slipped into a dream.

She was outside with a man. The surroundings were unfamiliar to her; the small earth toned mountains speckled with small green trees. She could feel she was with Tony, though it didn't look like him, and she knew being with him was forbidden. The scene switched. She held an infant and a man she seemed to know took it from her. Instead of trying to get the baby back, she walked away. But she knew he was going to kill her baby. Why didn't she stop him?

She tried to wake herself up, but felt so deep in a hole she couldn't pull herself out enough to open her eyes. Within moments she was in another dream.

She walked over to her dresser and picked up her antique mirror. In it she saw a reflection. Was it her? The woman was very old, her dark skin leathery and creased from years of sun and expression. Candace looked at the eyes staring back at her—not her own—and feelings of sadness overcame her. "I have to call Louisa," she thought within her dream. She picked up her cell phone off the dresser, where she always left it, but couldn't dial the number. She looked back in the mirror at the old woman.

As she tossed and turned, images of the baby and the old woman cycled in and out of her mind's eye for what seemed like an eternity. She finally broke free from the grip of whatever dream state she was in, and jerked herself up in bed. She quickly turned on the light, as if afraid of the dark. She looked around the room and at the antique mirror that rested on the dresser. She then looked for her phone where she left it, also on her dresser, but it was gone. As she stepped out of bed to look for it, she felt a thud next to her foot. Her phone had fallen to the floor. She picked it up and looked at it. Had she tried to call Louisa?

* * * *

Mondays can be bad enough when you've had a good weekend, but when you have a bad one? It was all Louisa could do to get herself into the office the following Monday morning. As she drove to work, she replayed her conversation with Candace over in her head and wondered if this was the straw the finally broke her: was it time to leave social work once and for all?

She walked into the office and tossed her scarf, gloves, and Ojo notebook on the table. She was going to take a look at it over lunch since she and Malory would be leaving in a week. The papers in the pocket slipped out, getting out of order, but she left the mess for later. Susan, her assistant, wasn't there yet, so she turned on all the lamps and her favorite guitar and cello CD, just what a woman needed to have playing in the background when writing a grant.

She went back into her office and immediately went to her e-mail to see if she had heard back from Cyndy. Bingo! The response was there. As she opened it and clicked "print," she heard the office door open and shut. Susan immediately came back to her office.

"Morning Louisa! How was your weekend?"

"Yucky," said Louisa, and turning to Susan, she relayed what happened over the weekend.

"You're kidding," said Susan with disgust. "How could child welfare justify sending him home like that?"

Louisa shrugged. "Candace should be here soon. Maybe she has more information."

Susan sat down in the chair across from Louisa's desk, and wiggled out of her bulky coat. "Listen. I read something last night. It was about people who have drowned in another life having asthma. It made me think of you."

"I must be in the twilight zone right now," said Louisa, "Listen to what I was just printing off."

The office door opened and closed again and they heard Candace toss her things on her desk. "Where is everybody?' Candace called.

"Back here," said Louisa and Susan in unison.

They waited for a response. Susan called again, "Candace?"

Candace slowly walked into Louisa's office holding a tan piece of paper; the brochure from Posi that had slipped out of Louisa's folder. Her hands were trembling and her face was pale. "What is this?" she asked.

"It's a brochure from New Mexico," said Louisa. "Are you okay?"

Candace sat down in the chair next to Susan. "I had these dreams, or something like dreams, when I was going through chemotherapy. It was like I was looking at a shadow box. Each of the squares was a room. It happened again last night, for the first time since the cancer. It looked just like this," she said, holding up the brochure which had a picture of a cross section of a pueblo.

Louisa felt the familiar tingle up her spine and looked down at the answer to the question she had sent the psychic. "Candace, there's a long story I need to tell you, but in a nutshell it involves what I believe to be past lives in New Mexico. I sent a question about it to a psychic and just got her response."

"What did it say?" asked Susan.

Louisa turned back to her computer and read the e-mail:

"Louisa,

I do see connections to you and a past life.

What I get is…First I saw a male and female in a past life – adults. And the female was drowned and the drowning was a murder.

But then Spirit showed me another picture. A picture of a family of four. A male and a female, and male and female child.

Then I saw the male taking a child and drowning it. I saw a picture that there was something wrong, and the male thought drowning the baby would make things better, or was the right thing to do. Like maybe the child was sick, or there wasn't enough food or water??? I don't know. So it wasn't in hatred but was a hateful act.

Then the woman clammed up after that. She was cold and withdrawn the rest of her life. She was distant from her husband whom she knew did this, but she either couldn't or didn't stop him. She was fearful of justice and that the deed would be found out by others. She lived in secrets then.

In the connection to now, these are aspects of your past soul trying to equalize or balance; to cancel out the past and move on from it. Sort of like a healing.

Spirit says that the people in both these past lives are players in the past and in the now for you."

"Both these past lives?" Louisa sat back in her chair with her hands over her mouth. "The one who drowned and the one who killed the baby were different people. Two different people—three counting Adelina. Susan, do you see? She just recounted the dream I had years ago about the woman who was drowned, and then the dream about drowning a baby!"

"What dream about drowning a baby? You didn't tell me that one." said Susan.

"Oh my god," said Candace.

Louisa looked at Candace, whose face had gone pale. "What?"

"I had a dream last night that someone took my baby and killed it," said Candace. "I didn't stop him. The dream went on, but I remember thinking within it that I needed to call you. Somehow my phone was in my bed—like I got up and picked it up off the dresser."

Candace looked at the brochure again and ran her finger across the picture of the pueblo. "Louisa?"

"Yes?"

"Can we e-mail that psychic?"

"I guess. What do you want to ask?"

"If I'm the mother of the baby that was drowned."

34

Malory sat with her feet propped on the coffee table in front of the fireplace. She and Louisa drove straight through the day before and arrived in Ojo Caliente after dark. It had been a wonderful, laid back day, and the smell of the piñon wood burning and the familiar New Mexico landscape comforted her.

While her life had changed on the outside over the past year, in many ways it seemed like it hadn't changed at all—which was both good and bad. With divorce came freedom but increased responsibility. She had found a job that wasn't a calling but an income. She had found a man that she loved, but at times did a double take to make sure she wasn't reliving her marriage with someone different. Why did it work that way? We pour our heart and souls into someone new and find the same issues staring us in the face.

Malory knew the answer, of course. She knew, deep down, that she was going to keep drawing similar circumstances into her life until, internally, she changed. But was it possible to do that while in a relationship? She hoped so, and shifted uncomfortably in her seat at the thought of the alternative.

Louisa had walked over to the hotel to check her e-mail. She was waiting on a response from the psychic about the baby that was drowned. Over the past few years, Malory had watched Louisa experience the discovering of other lifetimes and the work that facing herself required. Malory was the one person who totally grasped the "story" and was able to observe the way it intertwined with Louisa's life and experience. Within the memories of those other lifetimes were the very issues that Louisa needed to face, and in so doing, she gained understanding.

Louisa always said Malory was her "guide," and while Malory wouldn't have missed the ride for the world, she wanted her own understanding. Everyone has access to other parts of Self, right? She was ready to understand her own issues and relationships, and to know which patterns needed to be broken.

She picked up her hot cup of coffee and closed her eyes as she smelled its aroma. When she opened her eyes, she looked at Louisa's pile of Ojo documentation and books sitting on the coffee table. She picked up "Seth" and flipped through the pages, skimming sections that were underlined until she came to a section that resonated.

> "Not only are you part of other independent selves, each one focused in its own reality, but there is a sympathetic relationship that exists…because of this relationship, your experience need not be limited by the physical perceptive mechanisms. You can draw upon knowledge that belongs to other independent selves. You can learn to focus your attention away from physical reality, to learn new methods of perception that will enable you to enlarge your concept of reality and greatly expand your own experience.

> It is only because you believe that physical existence is the only valid one that it does not occur to you to look for other realities. Such things as telepathy and clairvoyance can give you hints of other kinds of perception, but you are also involved in quite definite experiences both while you are waking and while you are asleep.

> The so-called stream of consciousness is simply that- a small stream of thought, images and impressions-that is part of a much deeper river of consciousness that represents your own far greater existences and experiences. You spend all your time examining this one small stream, so that you become hypnotized by its flow…Simultaneously, these other streams of consciousness go by without your notice, yet they are very much a part of you. They represent quite

valid aspects, events, actions, emotions with which you are also involved in outer layers of reality.

You are not divorced from these other streams of consciousness, only your focus of attention closes you off from them…You can learn to look through (your stream of consciousness) and beneath it to others that lie in other beds of reality…The point is that you are only limited to the self you know if you think that you are.

Now in moments of solitude you may become aware…You may at times hear words or see images that appear out of context with your thoughts... Some of these may involve thoughts of what you would call a reincarnational self, focused in another part of history as you know it. You may instead "pick up" an event in which a probable self is involved, according to your inclination, psychic suppleness, your creativity, your desire for knowledge. In other words, you may become aware of a far greater reality than you now know, use abilities that you do not realize you possess, know beyond all doubt that your own consciousness and identity is independent of the world in which you now focus your primary attention."[7]

Malory recalled countless times that she had seen flashes of a face, familiar yet unknown, while drifting off to asleep, dreaming, or in quiet meditation. Are these other realities or streams of consciousness? And hasn't everyone had experiences of that nature yet we disregard them? She read on.

"Now the ego acts as a dam to hold back perceptions, not because it was meant to…but simply because you have been taught that the purpose of the ego is restrictive rather than expanding. (The ego) cannot relate to a reality that you will not allow it to

---

[7] (Roberts, pp. 90-92)

perceive. These other existences of yours go on quite merrily whether you are waking or sleeping, but while you are awake ordinarily you block them out. In the dream state you are much more aware of them…"[8]

Malory closed the book and buoyantly sat up to put it on the table. She felt a twinge of excitement in her stomach. She had made the decision: it was her turn. Her turn to discover the layers of her existence. Her turn to be happy, celebrated, and desired. It was time to stop focusing her life on helping other people get their acts together because her play was waiting for her to take part in it. Yes, it was time.

She took her coffee cup to the sink and headed back to the bedroom to get dressed for dinner. She looked at the clock. Louisa had been gone a while— too long. She decided she'd give her another ten minutes before she went looking for her.

* * * *

Louisa had read the response from Cyndy. It was brief, just like the straightforward question she and Candace had sent a few days earlier.

Hi Louisa,

I did meditate yesterday and asked spirit about the past life issues.

Yes, Candace Stevens was with you in a past life in NM area.

Yes, you were the male that drowned a child.

The soul, known now as Candace, never got over it in the past life. Almost went crazy with guilt and sadness. The male went along with life and really didn't understand why she was so distraught. He was never prosecuted or penalized for the act.

---

[8] (Roberts, p. 95)

Strong messages yes you were partners and parents
of a drowned child.

Peace

Cyndy

Louisa felt nauseous and broke into a cold sweat. She walked outside and sat on the steps, hoping the brisk air would help the feeling pass, but felt the urge to head north, which is how she ended up in the car. She turned off the main highway and saw where she wanted to be: Hupobi, its flat surface so obvious to her now. As she drove the curved road, it called to her as it came in and out of view. Tears streamed down her cheeks, while the image of the baby being held under flowing water passed in and out of her mind's eye.

The sun was setting and reflected off the cliffs that were now on the east side of the river. She felt a beckoning again, similar to what she felt during their second trip to Ojo. That beckoning led her to the river at the base of Hupobi, unaware of its existence or the meaning it would later hold for her. But this time she felt the need to go farther west. It was so strong she couldn't help but follow it, and Isaac and Caleb were somehow a part of her reason.

She made her way around a curve and saw a cow standing in the middle of the road, causing her to slam on her breaks. What was she doing anyway? Malory would worry if she didn't get back soon, so she turned around and headed back for Ojo.

Thunder Cloud

35

The elders sat in the circular kiva waiting for direction from the chief or his wife. The head mother stared at the ground, unwilling to fully face the decision that was being made. When she finally looked up, their faces turned to her, as if waiting for her to speak.

"I feel I must defer to Sun Breath as the holder of visions," she said quietly.

"I can only share my visions. I cannot make decisions. That is for this council to decide," said the priest.

Neither the chief nor his wife spoke. How could they? This was their daughter and a grandchild. Actions against either were decisions they would not be able to make themselves.

Another of the elders spoke up again. "This situation must be kept between council members, or we could lose all authority."

"I agree," said another.

Flower Morning's parents both took deep breaths and sighed in relief. "And what of the child?" questioned the chief.

The group sat in silence, no one wishing to speak.

"Well?" he asked again.

"Chief. This is a difficult subject and decision," continued the elder. "The child is tainted. Is she not, Sun Breath? How can we let the child live knowing that she will one day rule our village?"

There were nods of agreements. Tears filled the head mother's eyes and she turned away.

"Priest Sun Breath, what do you suggest to this council?" asked the chief.

"The child's Spirit can be released to the Spirit World and be accepted. She is not the product of incest. But the Spirits may not be pleased if we allow this transgression. Is that a risk we are willing to take for our people? We have been blessed with rains, and the raiders have kept their distance. I say that the Spirits have been pleased with us. I am sorry Head Mother. I know this is difficult for you both who have taken good care of this village. I simply speak what I believe to be true."

The chief nodded. "Then it will be so. I will speak to Thunder Cloud," he said quietly.

* * * *

As he looked toward the doorway, Thunder Cloud saw the first glimpses of light coming through the cracks around the blanket that covered it. It was dawn, and he prepared himself for what lay ahead. His father-in-law and the priest had explained that the life of the baby was to be terminated. He and Flower Morning were to come up with a story of what happened to the child, and Sun Breath would prepare her for a proper burial and journey to the Spirit world.

When Thunder Cloud had returned from his meeting with the chief, he walked in the doorway and sat with his back slouched against the wall of their large room. How would he tell his wife? Any mother by nature would put up a fight. But her duty to her tribe; certainly she would put that first, wouldn't she?

He waited patiently for her return. When she arrived, he moved toward her. "Flower, I must speak with you of the child."

"No," she had responded.

"But we must talk about this,"

"My mother has spoken with me, Thunder Cloud. I don't care to discuss it with you."

With that exchange, he had left the Pueblo. He walked down the steep hill that led to the river. There he sat until the sun was close to setting, assuring himself that he would fulfill his duty as ordered.

When he returned, Flower Morning and the infant were already asleep. "Hello son," whispered Thunder Cloud as he knelt down. "Going to sleep early tonight?"

"Mother said I must. She didn't speak much this evening," he whispered.

Thunder Cloud nodded. "Go to sleep," he whispered and put his hand on his son's back. He then turned and looked at his wife, her eyes closed. Spreading out his blankets, he lay awake and stared at the first stars through the smoke hole in the ceiling.

The night was an eternity, and when he saw the purple haze of sunrise, Thunder took a deep breath and rubbed his eyes. Rolling over, he saw the baby girl swaddled on the blankets where Flower Morning had laid the night before. He sat up, looked around the room, and then pulled back the blanket that covered the door. There was no one out in the plaza yet, and no sign of his wife. He looked to the west, wondering where she went but knew why it was she had gone. He went to the sleeping infant and lifted her into his arms.

He climbed down the ladder, and before leaving the pueblo, stopped to look at the horizon. The sacred peaks to the east glowed in a deep pink hue, and he prayed to the Great Sprit that he would right this wrong and that their people remain in good favor.

Thunder walked down to the river where he sat the night before, but this time in a disembodied state, only somewhat aware of his surroundings and the feel of the ground as he trekked down the hill. In the distance, the rushing water echoed the movement of his emotions as they surged forward and retreated as his intellect took over.

When he reached the edge of the river and as it flowed over the rocks, he numbly unwrapped the baby, causing her to stir and wake. With silent resolve, he put her in the cold water. As she startled and waved her tiny arms and legs, he pushed her beneath the surface and closed his eyes.

Adelina
36

The moment before death—what does that feel like? She tried to imagine it, but couldn't. She wondered what it felt like for Antonio, and if he thought of her as he slipped into whatever lay between life and death.

It had been fifteen years since their last exchange of words, yet her reputation as Antonio's mistress followed her, placing her on the fringe of the small society they lived within. She thought she had known loneliness in her life, but she would come to know she had only skimmed the surface its depths.

A small smile tugged at her lips as she recalled Manuel's face. She didn't love him the way she loved Antonio, but for a time she wasn't alone. He saved her, or she at least felt he did. He needed someone to take care of him after his wife died, so he proposed an arrangement and she accepted. It grew into a different kind of love, and for the last five years of his life, she learned what it was like to have companionship.

She stood outside and looked to the east, taking in the view of the tree spotted mountains, characteristic of the river valley in which she had spent her entire life. The river was not far in the distance, and she closed her eyes listening to its movement and feeling the breeze as it blew across her skin.

Her sight turned inward, but she was no longer lost in the emotion she found there. Isolation. Loneliness. Loss. She looked up toward the sky, noted it was very blue that day and recalled the countless nights she sat looking at the stars, waiting patiently for something in her life to change and the change never coming.

She had been alone again, and had been for more than three years. Three years of grieving what her life might have or could have been. Three more years of hunger and struggle to meet her most basic needs, and of feeling ostracized and alienated in the town she had lived in since she was a child. She was done.

She walked into the small, sparse house and sat down. The early afternoon sun came in through the small window and splashed across the dirt floor stained with the animal blood used to pack it down years before. She reached for a black and white photograph of her daughter and held it to her chest. The solitude of her life overwhelmed her and the emotional distance she felt earlier was gone.

She climbed onto the stool and placed the rope she had tied to the beam around her neck. She sobbed at the thought of no one noticing her absence. She closed her eyes tightly, and as she silently called to the God she had long ago lost faith in, she stepped off.

Louisa

37

She's in another body, running. She sees the sunlight filtering through the leaves on the cottonwood trees as they flutter in the breeze and the river on her left. He's behind her, breathing hard, and she pushes ahead as fast as she can, recognizing she is in the dream where the woman is going to be drowned. He reaches out and grabs her arm, and as he pulls her into the water, she turns and sees his face.

Louisa's eyes flew open and she tried to make sense of her dream. Dustin was the drowner? When was the last time she saw him? It was fifteen years ago at the Air Force base; she had been asked to come speak on behalf of United Way and saw him as she was leaving. It was almost surreal. They hugged as if they had been life long friends, but in reality they hardly knew each other. They were in sophomore honors English, and then would occasionally pass each other in the hall the last two years of high school. There was definitely some sort of draw between them, and Louisa knew he sensed it too. Funny how when you're young, any feelings toward the opposite sex are considered a "crush," but this was different than a crush. It was stronger than that. It was as if she knew him—and it frightened her.

* * * *

Twenty years sounds like a long time, but really, it's not. It had been twenty years since she graduated from high school, and her reunion was coming up in a few months. It had been twenty years since she and Matthew had first gotten together. Twenty years. Yet, here he was in her bathroom using a hammer to bust a tile around the base of the tub so he could replace the drain.

They—Louisa and Matthew—had been spending time together on occasion. It seemed in their history the two didn't really "date," and this was no different. But the reality she could now see was that years before, when she and Alan were still married and before she had even seen Matthew, she was having an emotional affair of sorts. No words of love or romance had to be exchanged for her to feel Matthew's friendship and support via the internet. And as Alan once said, they had unfinished business.

While there were undeniable parallels between Matthew and his counterpart Antonio, particularly in relation to Louisa, there were also some big differences. Like the fact that Matthew was on the floor in Louisa's bathroom fixing a drain. Louisa was pretty sure Antonio never would have done that. Neither would Alan, which made the gesture even more significant to Louisa.

Louisa closed her eyes, fearful the tile wall would shatter. "Okay, do it." She heard the sound of smashing tile, and snuck a peek. "It worked?"

Matthew smiled at her from where he sat on the floor in front of the tub. "I was a little scared too," he said, holding the hammer toward her. "Here. Release your frustrations and smash it."

She did as she was told, and with every hit to the tile she felt herself getting in touch with her latent aggression—and there had to be tons of it. Harder and harder she pounded, until the mesh on the back of the tile was all that was left.

"Let's take that hammer from you now," Matthew said, playfully acting cautious.

"That felt really good," said Louisa.

"Yeah, I could tell," he said laughing. "I imagine some of that aggression was toward me."

"There's a high probability of that," she said as she handed over the hammer.

He pulled out the mesh, lay down on his stomach, and reached his hand into the hole to unscrew the pipe and drain. "Okay. Hand me the new piece," he said, and she gave him the pipe and drain that would replace the old one. "I'll hold my hand here to see if any water leaks through if you'll turn it on."

She turned on the water and looked down at him with her fingers crossed.

"I think we got it," he said and smiled up at her. "Let's put in the replacement tile."

She knelt down and put the tile in the hole. "It fits perfectly. Wow. That drain's been broken for almost two years."

"So what's next on the list? I'm not here very often, so you need to take advantage of me while I am," he said, affectionately patting her knee.

"You fixed the light fixture, the back door and this, so I think you've done enough," she said bending over from her spot on the floor and giving him a hug. "As independent as I am, I guess sometimes I need a man."

He laughed his normal boisterous, jovial, laugh that was always music to her ears. "You don't need a man, Louisa. You're an oak tree, remember?"

"What?"

"Remember what I told you years ago? You're like a big oak tree. Impervious to all that's around you. Shit happens, and it just bounces off of you."

"I think your perception of me may have been a bit erroneous. Nothing you did back then 'bounced off' of me," she said, standing and extending a hand to pull him up. "But we don't need to go there right now."

"I'm sorry," he said and pulled her into a hug.

She welcomed his embrace, and as she did, she thought about how long she had waited: for him, for an apology or acknowledgement. And in that moment she realized it didn't matter. The reconciling that needed to be done had been done within her over the past five years. "Thank you," she said.

But apparently she had more to understand and experience, or so it seemed. Or perhaps it was a test, because later that night, Louisa sat on her bed with her journal in her lap. She wiped the tears from her eyes, and began to write.

Journal Entry

April 2006

Matthew was here today. We met for lunch and when I told him I had maintenance projects to work on, he offered to come help me. I was overwhelmed by his kindness.

But the evening ended badly. I'm not sure what happened, but all of the sudden he was lashing out at me. While some is because I'm not in a position to be with him, I can't help but think that some of it's because I got married to someone else in the first place. Our dynamic was always that I waited and was available when he wanted me—and as far as I'm concerned, not just in this lifetime. When I think about when we were young, I see that he set the terms of our relationship: what we were, when we saw each other. It sickens me a bit to think I allowed it. My lack of availability when I was married, and now because of the kids, is a violation of the dynamic.

I know Matthew well and know I may not hear from him again for a long time. But while I'm hurt, I'm not devastated like I used to be. I think I've figured out that, at least when it comes to me, Matthew leaves. He comes into my life and I get to feel the comfort of his love, and then he leaves.

But I now know that love simply "is," regardless of how we think a relationship should look and I have a choice in how I participate and perceive what is happening. I see that Matthew is my teacher. Every time he leaves, I have the opportunity to respond differently than I have in the past. Those changes in me give me strength, and while I feel abandoned by him, I know that I'm going to be okay.

A friend once told me she read that life lessons don't go away once you learn them, because they are life lessons. I'd like to think that Matthew and I could change our karmic patterns, but I can only apply my awareness to myself. Until I master that, I will just keep telling myself I am not alone and I will pray for an inner peace.

38

She is in a place with a lot of small rooms. She feels aware of Dustin's presence, though it isn't Dustin, and she is looking for him. She then finds herself lying on the ground where she has been asleep. He is next to her and she is struck by the comfort of his presence.

Louisa woke up and the feeling of a deep connectedness penetrated her awareness, odd because he killed her. *Interesting; they were close.*

* * * *

Malory sat in the booth at the Thai restaurant waiting for Louisa. In front of her she had her plate of food as well as a plate of rice and veggies for Louisa. There was a woman who was also a patron of their favorite Thai buffet that they referred to as "The Broccoli Lady." She shamelessly took every last piece of broccoli out of the broccoli and cabbage mixture that Louisa loved, so Malory took care of it before either of them arrived.

It was an exceptionally warm day for late May. Her blouse felt snug and uncomfortable, and her high heeled sandals were pissing her off. She hated that she was in work clothes, and that she had to work at all for that matter. Nothing felt right in her life. Was Mercury in retrograde?

When Louisa walked in, Malory felt the water works starting in her eyes. Louisa could have this affect on her. God love the poor man who owned the restaurant; so often had she been crying over lunch with Louisa, he had to think she was the most unstable woman in the world.

Louisa slid into the booth and reached across the table to take Malory's hand. "What is it honey?" she asked.

"Just life. It makes me tired," Malory said, unrolling her napkin to wipe her eyes.

Louisa nodded empathetically. "You've had a lot of change in your life over the past year or so: a divorce, a new relationship, a new job. I admire you for charging ahead, but I don't know that you've dealt with your feelings yet."

"I can't. I just can't right now," said Malory, wiping her eyes. "I just wish we were sitting outside in New Mexico."

"I do too," Louisa said with a gentle smile. "We will be in about four months. Do you remember the commitment you made to yourself last time we were there? That you were ready to understand your own negative patterns? Maybe these feelings are part of that—it's not always pretty, you know."

"Maybe I can deal with my feelings when we're there," said Malory, wiping her eyes.

"Yeah, just keep pushing them down until October, okay? If they don't completely eat through your insides before then, you can let all your grief and sadness out while we're there. It would be a most memorable trip. We'll call it 'Malory's Meltdown.' Sound good? I'm all for it—I'll even bring the Kleenex."

Malory laughed through her tears. "Distract me from my pity party," she said. "What's going on with you?"

"Speaking of New Mexico," Louisa said with raised eyebrows as she picked up her fork and stabbed a piece of broccoli. "I had a dream and I think I know who the 'drowner' is."

"Get out of here! Tell me everything," Malory said, perking up as Louisa told her the dream about Dustin.

"I think I'm going to consult Cyndy," said Louisa.

"You can do that," said Malory as she took a swig of Diet Coke, "but she's just going to tell you you're right."

"Maybe not," said Louisa, opening her straw. "Thanks for getting my plate by the way—you know who just walked in."

Malory glanced over and saw the Broccoli Lady at the buffet and smiled, then continued. "When are you going to accept that you have been doing a pretty good job being your own psychic?"

"You're right, but a little affirmation does my mind some good."

When Louisa got home, she turned on her computer and checked her personal e-mail. She went through and deleted the spam and came across one from an address she didn't recognize. The subject read "Hi Louisa." She opened it.

"Oh my God," she said aloud. It was an e-mail from Dustin. *This can't be for real.* Flustered, she got up to get the phone to call Malory, turned back around, went back for the phone, then turned around again to at least read the e-mail first.

"Hi, Louisa, it's Dustin. Glad to see you finally found the website for the twenty year reunion..." Talk about synchronicity. She e-mailed him back and then went to Cyndy's website. Her question was short and to the point. "Did a person from my youth named Dustin Cox and I share another life? If so, was he a male that drowned me (as another female) in a river in New Mexico?"

Cyndy's response came the next day.

> *Hi Louisa,*
>
> *I did ask spirit about you and Dustin. Here are the pictures and messages in no particular order.*
>
> *I asked did DC and Louisa share a past life.*
>
> *Yes.*
>
> *Then I see a picture of three people—like you him and another—maybe a baby, friend, or lover. Unsure which, but you shared a lifetime with him in which*

there was a conflict about three people or three hearts.
I see three hearts like all torn up and bleeding...

So something that involved three people and sad
and hurt and sorrow.

Then I asked did the soul of DC in a past life drown
a woman who is now Louisa? Yes. But again I get three
people...three hearts. Maybe you were pregnant at that
time or there was somehow another person involved
too...

Was she surprised? No. She could honestly say that after the past several years, she was finally beginning to get the hang of it. Did she see a pattern about a possible clandestine relationship; a child? You bet. And more than the death by drowning, it was those parallels that stayed with her.

Louisa's dreams would continue to ebb and flow in the background of life and summer activities with Isaac and Caleb, but the more they occurred, the deeper she became aware of her connection to Dustin. And while she couldn't explain it, she suspected he was feeling it too. Maybe it was time to tell him.

* * * *

When Dustin got the e-mail from Louisa saying she wanted to share something with him, but first asked if he had "fluidity of the mind," he had no idea what he was in for. She presented the information to him in stages like a teacher would present the steps of a math problem, starting with a story about a psychic who had contact with one of her children before he was born. It went from that to a story about New Mexico, past lives, and that she believed he drowned her in another lifetime—which was confirmed by the psychic who had contact with her child before he was born. She even sent him a copy of the psychic reading.

Dustin was a pragmatic person by nature, so it wasn't necessarily that he didn't believe her so much as it was that he didn't know if he believed in anything. Some of this was pure retaliation from his own religious upbringing which was shoved down his throat with an intensity parallel to a child being forced to eat liver; once grown, they'll never eat it again.

But what Louisa told him intrigued him, if for no other reason than he had felt an odd connection to her since he was a teenager. He rarely saw her when they were young, except the one time they had a class together, but when he did, he felt a strange sensation in the pit of his stomach—it wasn't normal.

He remembered that feeling years later when he ran into her at, of all places, the Air Force base. He had gone into the military immediately after high school—long story there—and went on to live in Alaska. He had just come back to Oklahoma and of all people to run into, he ran into her. He wanted to call her after that, an indicator that she didn't make him quite as uneasy as she did when he was fifteen, but perhaps still uneasy enough to keep him from picking up the phone. Now that he was past it, they lived in different states.

After their e-mail correspondence about New Mexico, he started having strange dreams himself. They didn't seem anything like the ones Louisa described, but they were out of the ordinary for him. One even caused him to fall out of bed. In it he was sitting on a roof, and a massive beam of light was coming toward him. Instead of dodging it, he let it carry him away and he rode on it until he began to slide off. Then, with a jolt, he woke up as he landed on the floor. He wondered if he would have even noticed his recent dreams if he hadn't been in contact her.

So was it possible he and Louisa had known each other in another time? It would certainly explain some things, like why he had felt uneasy around her and why he had so often thought about her over the years. But killing someone? The person he was today wouldn't be capable of that, or so he thought. When he asked Louisa if it scared her, she said no; that perhaps they had come into this life with recognition of one another, explaining why they had felt drawn to each other when they were young, and maybe a safe, distant connection was what they were supposed to experience to begin to deal with what they had shared together. Who knew, maybe she was right. Regardless, it would be good to see her the following week at the reunion.

39

Louisa walked into her closet, kicked off her black sandals and tossed the black silk shrug she wore over her dress onto the shelf. The cushion of the carpet felt good against her feet, now sore from a night of dancing at her high school reunion. She turned on the bedside lamp and plopped down on the bed next to Baxter the cat and leaned against her pillows. It was two o'clock in the morning and she was wide awake.

The kids were with Alan for the night, something they rarely did, and the house felt empty. She felt a twinge of sadness and, trying to hold it at bay, pulled the cat into her lap. "You're my loyal companion, aren't you Baxter," she said. "You've slept by my side for fifteen years." Baxter purred loudly and then moved to curl up in the crook of Louisa's arm.

She felt alone and thought about Matthew who had, so predictably, ignored the few attempts she made to contact him after their argument. What was his problem anyway? Before he left that night three months earlier, he had the audacity to criticize her life choices—getting married to Alan and having children with him, specifically. As if his life choices were superior? But ultimately she knew better. It was a temper tantrum; he was hurt and wanted her to hurt too, so he went after what was most precious to her. She had a long history of being forgiving and unconditionally loving with Matthew, so why was he so punitive?

She tried to shift her focus. It really had been a great night, and it was going to be hard to come down off of the high. She and her best friend from high school, Kay, had ridden together. When they arrived at the country club, they were both nervous in a funny, adolescent sort of way. Oddly enough, they didn't recognize anyone at first- except the band group of course, which had kept in touch sporadically over the years. Among the many old friends she had seen, she saw Dustin, but the music was too loud to have a good conversation. If he wasn't leaving town they could have grabbed a cup of coffee, but his flight was leaving early the next day. Both pulled in different directions, he gave the back of her arm a squeeze and nodded when she told him she'd try and catch up with him later. When she went to look for him before she left, he was already gone.

Maybe that was part of why she felt sad; her brief contact with this person she felt was so strongly linked to her "past." While her knowledge of him was quite minimal, there was something deeper than that; an inexplicable familiarity that she knew may always resonate within her being. It was in that moment that Louisa knew a part of her, the part that was Ma-Wi-Taa, loved him, and she began to understand that, in spite of their tragic ending, it was those positive feelings that carried forward.

Tears filled Louisa's eyes as she felt the connection with Dustin surge through her. It made no sense that she was crying, but she was. She stepped off the bed and pulled off her dress, grabbed a t-shirt and pulled down the covers. She put two pillows next to her, one for Isaac and one for Caleb, and slipped into bed.

As she closed her eyes, she wondered if she would ever see Dustin again or if their business with one another was complete. If they had explored their connection to one another years before, how might her life had been different? And what dynamics would they have played out with one another? Then she stopped herself. All was unfolding as it should, and she had no regrets: about Matthew, about Alan, about her marriage. She had trust, and with that last thought, she silently sent a message of peace and gratitude to all three of these men that had, in their own ways, touched her life.

* * * *

And so it happened that close to five years after Louisa's first trip to Ojo and the dream of a drowning that laid the groundwork for a journey beyond her imagining, the pieces of Ma-Wi-Taa's story, her life and death, had finally come together.

Ma-Wi-Taa
40

She sat with her eyes closed as she felt the cool air blowing across her skin. She opened her eyes to see the late afternoon sky through the intermingling of gold and green leaves on the trees, and then down at her abdomen. Placing her hand there, she felt the small bulge that had recently started to form. She knew she didn't have much time before he came back. She took the small cracked pot in her hands, feeling how hot it still was. She closed her eyes, said a prayer to the Great Spirit, and drank the mixture.

She heard the deep thud of stomping hooves.

"They're coming," he said, jumping off his horse and grabbing what belongings they had and threw them in a pack. "We must go."

"How soon will they be here?" she asked.

"Two days, perhaps."

He explained that he had made his way over a ridge, and below saw De Vargas's troops, now bigger by the hundreds than months earlier, setting up camp in a valley just a few hours to the southwest. Passing a lone trader on his way north, he learned that the Spanish had taken most every Pueblo, had hundreds of captives, and most recently had battled the Jemez on a high butte to the south. The battle was a success for the Spanish. Always strong allies to Ma-Wi-Taa's people, the survivors were told they could live if they agreed to help conquer the Tewa, the last remaining refugees, still atop Black Mesa.

The two started their journey south until it was dark. "We will go to El Paso, where it is safer," he said.

"I cannot leave my home," Ma-Wi-Taa replied.

He looked at her with disbelief. "If you live, you'll be a slave—what of the baby?"

She put her hand on her stomach, and closed her eyes. She was beginning to feel the cramps, and knew by morning she will have miscarried. "I must rest," was all she said.

He put a pack on the ground for her, and they both laid down, his arm across her. Her sleep was shallow, and during the night her pains increased. She curled up on her side, and tried to contain her moans as her uterus contracted. It would be over soon. Black Mesa was in the distance, and she thought of her people. She knew it was time to leave this man she had loved and warn them. It had been four moons since she left. She had no idea then what those months would hold for her; fear, passion, love, and a deep peace with someone who should have been her enemy. The intensity of their feelings for one another had consumed them, but now she had to force herself to break away and do what she had initially intended: fight for her home.

At first daylight, she knelt over and gently kissed him goodbye, and when she stood, she felt blood trickle down her leg. Still cramping, she was not a day's walk from the mesa.

She traversed the river, as she generally did, and finally stopped when the sun was high. She could see Black Mesa in the distance, and would have to make her way around it to access the only trail to the top.

She pulled her dress up over her knees and waded into the river. She scooped some water into her cupped hand to drink, and then started to wash the blood from her legs. She heard a horse coming from behind and she turned to see the man she loved as he led the animal splashing through the shallow water. He stared in horror at her blood-stained dress and legs.

She saw desperation building in his eyes until he closed them and finally spoke. "Where are you going?"

"Home. I must warn my people."

"You'll be raped, killed. Why? And the baby?"

She looked down at her blood stained dress. "I couldn't bring a baby into life—not now. The Spanish are conquering us. I couldn't. There would be no life for it."

He stood, speechless.

"I must go," she said, stepping away from him.

He grabbed her around the waist and held her tightly. She struggled to get away, and saw a look in his eyes she had never seen before, and her uneasiness turned to fear. "Please-you are hurting me," she said, but he wouldn't let her go. Panicking, she leaned down and bit his wrist as hard as she could, causing him to let go of her arm, and she broke away from his grip.

She turned, stumbling back through the river, now shallow, and started running as fast as she could down the other side. She heard him splash through after her, but kept running, navigating the rocky terrain. Her awareness was pulled toward the autumn leaves fluttering in the breeze as the sun shone through them, her tribe, high on the mesa in sight, but out of reach, and the pain in her lower abdomen. She took in every detail around her, trying to figure out where to go next, and had no time to think about the rage and desperation that turned the man she had trusted into the predator she was running from.

She heard him gaining on her, and felt his hand reach out and brush her sleeve. Pushing as fast as she could ahead, he grabbed her while letting out a deep scream and pulled her toward him and into the water. Forcing her under, he had one hand on her head and the other on her shoulder as he pushed her down. She thrashed, trying to get up for air. She felt the weight of his body as he leaned in, holding her under. In a slow motion, she observed her own thrashing. The cold water rushed on her face and in her hair, and her knee scraped the river bottom as she grabbed at his hands to get him to release his grip. Her eyes open, she caught a glimpse of his dark hair and the sleeve of his white shirt above the surface of the river.

As her fight subsided, she was taking in water, and she called out to him in her mind. *You think you can harm me, but you can't.* As her consciousness began to drift, her body went limp in the river.

Dragging her by her arm, he pulled her out of the water and rolled her onto her back. A deep, long, painful cry carried across the landscape and echoed back. He fell to the ground on his knees, and realizing what he had done, he put his arms around her and pulled her limp body to his chest.

Louisa

41

He drags her across the ground by her arm and rolls her over onto her back, with a thump. Louisa, somewhat aware of her own surroundings lying in bed, flips over from her side to her back in the same moment as the woman in the dream. THUMP— as if in two places at once. She opens her eyes and looks around the bedroom. She sees the light from the clock and the dim light coming in the bedroom door. She feels the cat next to her and the dog against her legs.

She's dizzy. "Something isn't right," she says to herself. "Am I dying?" In that instant, all her senses go black. She is surrounded by complete darkness; a deafening silence. She knows she's dead and between places, but if she waits a few moments, a light will come into view, won't it? "Wait a minute—I'm dead? How can this be?" She starts to recall the dream she was having before she opened her eyes. "No, not me," she says to herself, "it's her. This is her death." With the realization, the room slowly fades back into view. She sees the clock; the light from the doorway. Then, as if the volume was slowly turned up, she begins to hear the fan and the sounds of her house.

Unsure if she could move, Louisa moistened her dry lips and tried to swallow. She wiggled her fingers and toes, and felt the heaviness of her body against the bed. As she cautiously took a breath, she tried to assimilate what had just happened.

* * * *

"You relived her death?" Malory asked, sitting in the porch swing on Louisa's front patio the following Saturday morning.

"Or something like that," Louisa said, looking over her mug of Bailey's and coffee from where she sat in a chair opposite Malory. "It wasn't like the rest of my dreams. I was myself, having this experience in what seemed to be an 'in between' place. I don't know that I've fully recovered yet." She sat back and thoughtfully stared out over the garden. "You know, this year has been a big one, as far as this whole story goes. Two deaths, both drowning, revealed to me. It's a bit much if I think about it."

"Louisa, it's taken five years for this story to come together. God, how time flies. So she never made it back to Black Mesa. What do you think happened to him- after he drowned her? Do you have a gut feeling?" asked Malory, gently rocking the swing with the toes of her right foot.

Louisa shook her head that she didn't and smiled. "Maybe it will someday be revealed to Dustin."

"Do you fully grasp all the parallels between you and these other selves? There are so many, in different forms. I wish we had a flow chart."

"You and the flow charts," said Louisa.

"I can't help it—I'm visual," said Malory, pulling her legs up and crossing them in the bench. "Let's start with the many 'not getting air' issues. You have asthma in this life, the Tewa woman was drowned, then drowning the baby."

"And Adelina hung herself," Louisa added, gesturing toward Malory with her mug. "And the Jewish lady. Remember when I was pregnant with Caleb?"

Malory shook her head that she didn't. "Another one?"

"It actually started in my early twenties; the memories that came through during a meditation. I was in the body of a young girl, and I could see the table in the kitchen and yellow walls. Then the scene changed and she was an adult in a small market. There was a man wearing a cap and he had long curls of hair." Louisa used her finger to mark a curl on her cheek. "It wasn't something I was familiar with at that point. I didn't think much of it until I was at the Holocaust Museum in D.C. several years later and saw a picture of a man with the same curls. A few months later when I was pregnant with Caleb, I had a dream and found myself in a woman's body. She was naked and so were her two children. They were school age, and were clinging to her waist. They were being shoved, and there was a man, who was wearing a khaki shirt, and he shoved them aggressively. It felt like a Holocaust scene. I pulled myself out of the dream, horrified, and started sobbing. In that moment I knew why I had hard pregnancies. I didn't feel worthy of being a mother because I couldn't protect them. And here I am in a profession with the focus of protecting kids. It happened so quickly but had a huge impact on me, so I called Alan at work. He couldn't understand me and ended up getting in the car and coming home."

"The challenge of being in a marriage with Louisa," Malory said with a sigh.

"And clearly there are so many," said Louisa with a self deprecating humor. "Alan's probably right when he says no other man could handle me."

Malory giggled. "So this woman and her kids were gassed in a chamber?"

"I think so."

Malory kicked her feet up onto the stool in front of the porch swing and twisted her long, blonde hair up in a knot to get it off her neck. "Okay, we have the air/choking issues. You with asthma, the drowning woman and baby, the suicide, and now the Jewish woman and the gas chamber. You then have Adelina who lost her two children, the baby that had to be drowned, the Jewish woman and her children being gassed, and you in a career of child protection. You can't deny the parallels."

Louisa looked at Malory wide-eyed. "Don't forget the clandestine relationship pattern—yikes."

"I hadn't fully registered those—but you're right," Malory said returning Louisa's wide-eyed stare and smiling. "You know Louisa, you're not the same person you were even a few years ago."

"What do you mean?" Louisa asked.

"As someone who knows you intimately, I see these subtle but dramatic differences in how you respond to your life."

Louisa stared at the clouds that slowly drifted across the blue sky. Malory was right. "It's been quite a gift the Universe has given me."

"You've done the work, though, and not all of it has been pretty."

Louisa nodded quietly as she stared down at the ground. "It's our birthright, isn't it— to know other parts of our multidimensional selves?"

"I hope so." Malory said, and rolled her head to stretch her neck. "Louisa, would you mind working on my neck?"

"Of course not," Louisa said, putting down her coffee cup and stepping behind the porch swing where Malory sat. She put her hands on Malory's neck and began to feel around for tension. "Yep, I feel the problem. A little trigger point work and we'll have you good as new."

Louisa pressed her thumb into the side of Malory's neck while holding the weight of her head with the other hand. "You know, they were so different. Thunder Cloud—I don't know how to relate to him. In spite of what happened in his life, he feels fine to me. But Ma-Wi-Taa and Adelina? They were almost the antithesis of one another in how they lived their lives."

"*You think you can harm me, but you can't…*" Malory interjected.

"Exactly."

"Do you think you and Matthew are finished?" Malory asked, letting her body relax into Louisa's thumbs.

"I'm not sure," Louisa said, shifting Malory's head so she could rub the other side of her neck. "He's very significant to me and always will be. If we are meant to cross paths again, we will. There's no such thing as goodbye— I know that now."

"Do you still feel Adelina?" Marilyn asked.

Louisa looked thoughtfully at the last flowers in her garden in full bloom against the blue sky. "Yes," she said, "but I understand her now, and that I can't get entangled in her experience. That happened at first. Her end was such a hopeless one; no one to remember her, her body in an unmarked grave."

"No," said Malory. "There are rocks marking her grave. And you remember her, Louisa."

Louisa wrapped her arms around Malory and gave her a hug from where she stood behind the porch swing. "Yes. She is remembered."

42

A full year passed. Louisa and Malory once again made their way through northern New Mexico. Louisa had spent the last year writing about her experiences at Ojo Caliente, Adelina, Thunder Cloud, and Ma-Wi-Taa, and in her backpack were two copies of the manuscript. Where better than New Mexico, she thought, to read through it for the first time.

The sunroof was open and a cool autumn breeze caused their hair to dance about their faces. As they drove, they listened to Gordon Lightfoot, their official Ojo soundtrack, when "Rainy Day People," came on.

"Ah. Those rainy day people," Louisa said, shifting her body toward Malory as she rode in the passenger seat. "I think we each might need one of those."

"I think you're right," Malory said as Gordon sang in the background.

"Those rainy day people," Louisa said just behind the phrase as it was sung, "they know when it's time to call. They listen until they've heard it all because they've been down like you."

"And they don't care if you cry a tear or two," Malory added as she glance over at Louisa.

"They sure don't, God love 'em," said Louisa. "Look at this amazing landscape."

"Gorgeous."

"You know, Mal—rainy day lovers don't love any others."

"They don't. That wouldn't be kind."

"It sure wouldn't. They just wait around 'til we need them, I guess."

"I need one of those," said Malory, as she turned on the highway that led to the bridge where Louisa always had anxiety attacks. "You okay?"

"Oh my gosh, I am. I can breathe!" said Louisa.

Malory smiled. "That's progress, baby!"

"Malory, I think I'm going to be alone a while," Louisa said.

"Yeah, I think so too," Malory said. "But I think you're okay with it. I think your fears about ending up alone have been faced. You're like Judy in *Private Benjamin*."

"Huh?"

"Remember at the end of *Private Benjamin* when Judy walks out on her wedding? She walks down the road in her gown and she smiles, and you know that she figured out she's going to be just fine on her own."

"I do remember that," said Louisa.

"You're like Judy."

"Thanks Malory."

Malory turned Louisa's silver Subaru onto an unpaved road and the bags of groceries in the back toppled over on their sides. "Pretty bumpy," said Malory. "Your new car's getting broken in on its first trip to New Mexico. I sure do miss the van, though. It served us well on our many trips here."

"The Mazda. Oh, the places it took us. But oh, the toll all those miles took on it," said Louisa as she looked up and saw Black Mesa spanning in both directions. She placed her hand on her chest, breathing deeply.

"Are you okay?" Malory asked. "I know the drowning sight is pretty close to where we're staying."

"I'm okay. It feels right to be here right now. Hey, I forgot to tell you that I came across some information about a book of Tewa names while doing my research. There's a copy, it should be on the San Juan Pueblo. I called and asked if I could look at it. Do you mind if we go one day?"

"Not at all. What are you looking for?"

"I want to look at it and pick a Tewa name for Ma-Wi-Taa. But more than that, I remember the day I heard that name whispered in my ear, and I may be hoping for too much, but maybe it's actually a Tewa name."

Malory nodded as she saw the cattle gate for the drive. She hopped out and unlocked it and they drove up to a small adobe nestled at the base of the mesa. Complete silence surrounded them as they got out of the car, and after climbing the steps onto the porch, they stopped and looked at the view of the Jemez Mountains. "Incredible," Louisa whispered.

"It is," whispered Malory.

After carrying in the first load, they opened up the windows in the small, airy living room. The afternoon sun streamed through them as Black Mesa emanated its strength outside.

"Are you sad we aren't staying at Ojo?" Malory asked, walking toward the grocery sacks on the kitchen counter.

"No," said Louisa, pulling a loaf of bread and a bag of coffee out of a sack. "Ojo's priced working folk like us right out of the market."

"That's for sure," said Malory. "But I didn't know if you'd be sad because you feel Adelina so strongly there."

"I do feel her strongly when I'm there. But she feels okay right now. It's Ma-Wi-Taa's turn. I think that's why we ended up staying here."

"Speaking of it being Ma-Wi-Taa's turn, when will you be meeting Dustin?"

Louisa smiled. "We're meeting tomorrow, but only for a few hours." She handed Malory a head of lettuce to put in the refrigerator.

"Talk about synchronicity," said Malory, taking the lettuce. "His family reunion being in Red River the exact same dates we were here, at Black Mesa, a stone's throw from where he drowned her?"

"It's great, isn't it? Life unfolds in such a remarkable way."

"At least yours does," Malory said as she smiled.

"I'd say both of our lives do. Look where we're staying for the next three days. We're blessed."

"That we are," Malory nodded. "That we are."

The next morning as Louisa lay in bed, she looked out the window at Black Mesa and the purple dawn sky. She got out of bed, slipped her feet into a pair of slipper boots and walked into the bathroom and saw a mark on her face.

"Malory?" she called.

Malory came into the bathroom. "What's that splotchy red mark across your face?"

"I don't know. Isn't that strange?"

"No. You always have something happen either before, during, or after your trips here," said Malory.

"I guess it's better than losing an organ," said Louisa.

"No more of that please," said Malory, walking down the hall to the kitchen. "You're so *somatic*."

"Not by choice," Louisa said loudly. "Is your computer hooked up? I might check my work e-mail."

"Go ahead."

Louisa logged on and saw e-mails from Kara and Lea. Over the past few years, both had left their positions as Directors of their local child advocacy programs, and had e-mailed for personal reasons. She smiled at their timing. She then read several messages related to statewide discord related to work. When she finished, she walked into the kitchen and put the kettle on for some tea.

"How's the tribe behaving?" Malory asked.

"You're good!" said Louisa. "E-mails from Lea and Kara."

"They must have sensed you were in the homeland," Malory laughed.

"Exactly my thought—they always reach out, even when they don't know I'm here. And then there's conflict on the statewide scene."

"So the tribe's misbehaving— still acting out its experiment set in the 21st century, I see."

"We must be, yes, and I hope we get it right this time." Louisa pulled a mug out of the cupboard and poured water from the kettle on the stove. "But the drama takes on a whole new meaning when I look at it in that context."

Malory took a seat on the stool on the other side of the counter. "So," she said, "what's your plan this morning?"

"I think I'm going to drink this tea and then make the drive to Ojo. Do you want to join me?"

"I think I'll stay here," said Malory. "I sense you might need to make the trip alone."

"Yes," Louisa said, stirring some sugar into her tea. "I have some things I need to do."

Louisa finished her tea, grabbed her swimsuit, and drove fifteen minutes to the north. It was a cold October morning, and when the sun broke over the mesa, it intensified the golden cottonwoods that lined the river. When she pulled into the small town of Ojo Caliente, she slowed down and turned onto the drive that led to the back of the graveyard.

She got out of the car, walked over to a ridge and picked up a small rock to place with the others she had previously put on Adelina's grave. As she walked toward the grave, she crossed her arms to fend off the chill in the morning air. As she did, she felt Adelina gently touch her psyche, and in her mind she spoke to her. "Adelina?"

Louisa closed her eyes and felt the familiar tingle up her spine and the presence behind her shoulder. "He loved you, to the best of his ability for who he was at the time. He still does, now, through me, regardless of what form our relationship takes. It is real, and present, and significant enough to follow us through space and time." If Adelina could understand that sometimes love just "is," regardless of what our lives look like, it might help her. Or maybe, just maybe, Louisa's understanding would reach her and in multidimensional reality, she could in some way know it too.

Louisa knelt down to set the rock on the gravesite and rested her hand on the cold pile of rocks in front of her. She closed her eyes and felt the breeze on her face. She thanked Spirit for showing her Adelina and for opening her up to understanding what she and Adelina shared. With a quiet farewell until next year, Louisa walked back to her car and went on to the springs for a soak before she met Dustin.

* * * *

Dustin pulled his black truck onto the shoulder of the road. They walked down the small embankment and climbed through a barbed wire fence to get closer to the water.

"Now what?" he asked her.

"We need to be on that side. She was dragged in over there," said Louisa, pointing across the river.

"You mean it happened right here?" he asked, gesturing to the area with his hands.

Louisa nodded. "On that side."

"Are you sure?"

"Positive. I remember. She was running on that side of the river."

"Well, let's go," he said as he held open the barbed wire fence for her to climb back through, and then she did the same for him. They got in his truck, drove up the road and over the bridge to the other side.

They walked down the steep embankment to the fence that lined the area and they stood on the edge of a grove of old cotton wood trees. Louisa assessed the fence, made of a grid of metal with barbed wire on top and found it was impossible to climb. "Look at this. I can't climb this," she said. She looked over and saw Dustin had walked toward the river. "What are you doing?"

"Just looking to see if there was another way to get through to the river," he said. "Whoever owns this land went to great lengths to make it difficult to get through."

"They probably want to keep kids from partying down by the water," Louisa said, kicking an empty beer can. Dustin walked toward her as she sat down on the embankment. He sat down next to her as she continued to speak. "I'm just surprised that I can't get over there.

It seems like things generally open up for me. We can't mark her grave. "

"Look at the land," Dustin said, pointing to the erosion in front of them on the other side of the fence. "The river has been here—and very well may have been four hundred years ago. Who knows, we may be right on the spot, or at least close to it."

"The river has been here," she said thoughtfully.

"Something doesn't feel right, though," he said. "There's something more. I don't think this is the spot."

"It's the spot."

"But there's something, I can't explain it," he said.

"Well, she died, so her last imprint on physical reality was here. The man that you were continued on. You've got your own karma with this place—that's your deal," Louisa said smiling and nudging him affectionately. "I wonder what he did with her body?"

"People were probably looking for him."

"Yes, and then the Tewa were right over there," Louisa said, pointing to Black Mesa. "Do you think he just left her?"

"Life was different then. It was about survival. I don't know that we can even think from their perspective," Dustin answered. He stared contemplatively at the grove of cotton wood trees along the river, their autumn leaves fluttering in the breeze. Louisa sat quietly, lost in her own thoughts.

"So," said Dustin, "if there's no such thing as linear time and everything is happening at once, then they're alive right now."

"Yes, they are," said Louisa, excited that he grasped the magnitude of what she was feeling. She put her arm through his and looked at him. "And if there are multiple probabilities, there can be a different ending."

Dustin slowly nodded. "I can understand that you would want closure on this."

"Thanks," Louisa said, again feeling a twinge of sadness. "You and I being in this spot together is important. I really appreciate you driving down here to meet me."

Dustin's cell phone rang and he pulled it out of his pocket. "It's my sister," he said.

"Time for you to get back," Louisa said, standing.

He stood and took her hand and kissed it. "This is special."

"It is to me too," Louisa said, giving him a hug. They turned and walked back to the truck.

"I still think there is something more," Dustin said.

"For him there was," she said. "This is where your ride begins."

* * * *

That night, Louisa stood on the porch looking at the sky. The mesa was dark, but above it were more stars than she had ever seen, and the Milky Way poured itself across the sky. She was filled with uneasiness in a way she hadn't experienced since her first few trips to Ojo. When she went to her bed, she got under the covers and curled up, leaving the light on.

She drifted in and out of consciousness, aware of being in another body but in her own at the same time. She felt intense cramping in her dream, and hugged her abdomen tightly as she lay curled up under the covers. They were reminiscent of labor pains, and the woman in her dream stoically endured them.

Louisa slowly pulled herself out of the shallow sleep state and opened her eyes. The curtains were open and she could see the shadow of Black Mesa outside the window and the star-packed sky above it.

"Malory?" she called.

"What sweetie?" Malory said, rushing in. "Are you okay?"

Louisa sat up in bed and Malory sat next to her, taking her hand. "She was pregnant. Ma-Wi-Taa was pregnant. She terminated the pregnancy."

"She would have known how," Malory said quietly. "And it fits with the pattern."

"And Malory," Louisa continued. "She had a birthmark on her face. She was marked."

Malory reached over and gently touched the red mark across Louisa's face, smiling. "Yes, I believe she was."

The next day and a half day were spent enjoying the company of a best friend, reading her manuscript for the first time, and soaking in the springs. Louisa knew there was more happening though—a recalibration of sorts, as Ma-Wi-Taa made her presence known in this location she once called home.

As they made their departure from Black Mesa, Louisa turned and looked at its grandeur and smiled to herself. All was well with the part of her that was Ma-Wi-Taa, and she was filled with a sense of peace.

But before they left New Mexico, they had one more stop to make: the San Juan Pueblo. They turned onto the dirt road that led toward the co-op where Louisa had read about the book of Tewa names.

They pulled into the parking lot of a small building and got out of the car. Walking in, Louisa approached the vacant counter and studied the hand made jewelry and woven items while she waited for someone to help her, and Malory crossed the room to look at the items on display.

A Tewa woman dressed in jeans and a t-shirt appeared from a back room and looked at Louisa curiously.

"Hi," said Louisa. "I called a few days ago about a book you have on Tewa names."

"It's not for sale," said the woman.

"I don't need to buy it," said Louisa, shifting her weight from one leg to the other nervously. "I was hoping you could look something up for me."

The woman nodded, retrieved the book, and brought it to the counter. "Tell me the English version, and I'll find the Tewa name."

"Actually, this might seem odd," Louisa said, "but I have a word in mind and I wanted to know if by some chance it is a Tewa name."

The woman looked at Louisa curiously.

"It sounds like Ma-Wi-Taa."

The woman scanned the pages, and stopped herself short. "Oh. Here it is," she said. "Let me make sure I am reading it correctly." She took it over to an elder more familiar with the Tewa language.

"MaaWää'Ta'," the elder said, just as Louisa had heard it whispered in her ear years earlier.

"What does it mean?" Louisa asked.

"It means to be marked or written," said the elder.

To be written... Louisa felt a tingle up her spine. Her mind went to the previous day spent wrapped in blankets, looking out over the Jemez, and reading her manuscript.

"Thank you very much," said Louisa, and Malory crossed the room to meet her at the door.

Malory took Louisa's hand and squeezed it firmly. "To be written. Well, she has been."

"Yes," said Louisa as tears filled her eyes. "Yes, she has."

* * * *

Journal Entry

I once commented to Malory how bizarre it was that, if we have multiple lives, 'I' chose to have so many in one location.

"Don't you see?" she said. "The recognition had to be strong enough to punch a hole into this reality."

Punch a hole it did. As the years have passed since Alan, in his own intuitive way, sent me on my first trip to Ojo Caliente, I have continually been awed by the story that unfolded, and the way it paralleled and intersected with parts of my own experience. It turned my life upside down, and in addition to facing some of my deepest fears, I have begun to grasp that we all are the "good" and the "bad," the male, the female, the victim and the perpetrator. Each aspect of Self lives its own variation of the experience, taking that experience back to the totality.

Is it reasonable to say that if I share a soul with the individuals I came to know as part of myself, that to a degree their experience is my experience? I believe so. And I believe that I carried that experience into this lifetime; to deal with, to understand, and ultimately to heal. But most significant? I have learned a new depth of truth to ideas I have long held: Love is eternal. Life is eternal. I imagine that is my greatest gift, and it is one that is on offer to all of us.

As the months continue to pass, new dreams enter my awareness. I sense the Jewish woman I dreamt of who was brutally shoved with her children and I feel a name on the tip of my tongue. I dream of a location farther west than New Mexico, and in each of these dream fragments I come back with images of steep cliffs and canyons, a feeling of danger, and an overwhelming sense of Isaac and Caleb. My dreams reflect that inner world that seems so out of reach and I am inspired as pieces of that story creep into my awareness on the cusp of another journey west. I don't know what the end of the story will be, because I imagine there is no end. Rather, pieces will be revealed as Spirit deems me ready to further understand my place in All That Is.

Closing

So how did I start this story? Ah, yes, adventure. As a mother of two young boys who is the Executive Director of a small non-profit, adventure was something I could only think about in passing; in those brief exhausted moments before I fell asleep, or as I folded the laundry and changed the diapers. But I found adventure, or maybe I should say this adventure found me. It was internal, it was subtle, but it was life altering and it was real.

With a degree of spontaneity previously unknown to me, I later found myself in Arizona with Dustin. We met in Sedona and had spent the past two days exploring ruins of the Sinagua Indians, believed to have been absorbed by the Hopi now living on the mesas to the northeast.

The day was hot, but there was one more ruin to explore on my mental list. As I walked up the sidewalk to the visitor center and dropped my backpack off my shoulder, I caught a glimpse of my reflection in the window. In that moment, my arms were covered in goose bumps in spite of the one hundred and seven degree heat. It was her—the woman with the blue eyes who had beckoned me almost a decade earlier, staring back at me, and at once I understood. The woman was me.

I am Louisa. I am Adelina. I am Ma-Wi-Taa and Thunder Cloud. I am a Jewish woman who died with her two children, someone who lived farther west in the canyons of Arizona, and I imagine countless others. Self meets self, beckoning us to become more than we presently are, all that we can be, and to recognize that we are far more than we think.

Now there's an adventure for you.

Cited Works

Roberts, Jane. *Seth Speaks: The Eternal Validity of the Soul*. California: Amber Allen Publishing and New World Library, 1972.

ABOUT THE AUTHOR

Sheryl Marseilles has a Masters in Social Work and resides in Norman, Oklahoma where she raises her two sons. For twenty years she has worked at a child advocacy organization that speaks up for abused and neglected children in court. This is her first novel.

www.timelesswaters.com